Avidly Reads

Board Games

ERIC THURM

NEW YORK UNIVERSITY PRESS *New York*

NEW YORK UNIVERSITY PRESS
New York
www.nyupress.org

References to Internet websites (URLs) were accurate at the time of writing. Neither the author nor New York University Press is responsible for URLs that may have expired or changed since the manuscript was prepared.

Library of Congress Cataloging-in-Publication Data
Names: Thurm, Eric, author.
Title: Avidly reads board games / Eric Thurm.
Other titles: Board games
Description: New York : New York University Press, [2018] | Series: Avidly reads | Includes bibliographical references and index.
Identifiers: LCCN 2019006919| ISBN 9781479856343 (cloth : alk. paper) | ISBN 9781479826957 (pbk. : alk. paper)
Subjects: LCSH: Board games—Social aspects.
Classification: LCC GV1312 .T58 2018 | DDC 794—dc23
LC record available at https://lccn.loc.gov/2019006919

New York University Press books are printed on acid-free paper, and their binding materials are chosen for strength and durability. We strive to use environmentally responsible suppliers and materials to the greatest extent possible in publishing our books.

Manufactured in the United States of America

10 9 8 7 6 5 4 3 2 1

Also available as an ebook

To Sammy — time to uphold your end of our deal

Contents

1

ENTER THE MAGIC CIRCLE

On a stale Florida day at the end of March, my family languished in a hospital waiting room, staring intensely at nothing in particular. We'd waited in the haze of the hospital's lobby for several hours before being led up to the dimly lit waiting room. Eventually, we would be taken to my grandfather's bed. He was in the late stages of pancreatic cancer, and we had come to say good-bye.

The waiting room was a grim, foreboding space, covered in old magazines and dull, browned tile. The television sandwiched into a corner of the ceiling was set to a *Vanderpump Rules* marathon, airing all of the drama leading up to a reality TV wedding. We could have chatted about nothing to fill the time, but a pair of women were rooted in chairs, silently perusing their copies of *People*; as painful as our situation was, we didn't want to disturb other people in a similarly fragile state. And besides, there's not much you can say, sitting around waiting for death. So my brother, sister, and I did the only thing we could think of: we took a big, red cardboard box out of a tote bag, sidled up to the table at the center of the waiting room, and started setting up a game of *Catan*.

The three of us had been playing the game originally known as *Settlers of Catan* obsessively for over a year by this point, so we had all of the steps down cold, like a pit crew mechanically getting their car ready for a race. We fit together the skeleton of the board—six pieces of coast that create the outline of the island of Catan, filled in by hexagons representing the island's various resources. We knew the cost of building roads, settlements, and cities—the elements of your civilization. We knew the uses and abuses of each of the game's development cards. We even knew the particular circumstances under which it makes sense to trade resources: when one of us wanted to swap a lumber card for an ore, we would simply point or gesture without needing to speak. Save for the intermittent rolling of dice and the incidental wooden plunk of a road or settlement, there was no sound.

No games are *good* for waiting to say your final good-bye to a dying relative, but all things considered, *Catan* isn't a bad one. You can play without talking, if you need to—in theory, a game could play out entirely in silence, letting the dice and each player's individual choices guide the outcome. This also means *Catan* isn't overly competitive, unless you want it to be. The players can largely ignore each other if they so choose, instead focusing on their own strategies, whether that's building up cities and settlements or pursuing the floating Longest Road and Largest Army cards. More than anything, the *Catan* system is accommodating, which might partially explain why it's one of the most popular board games in the world, with more than eighteen million copies sold since its publication in 1995.

Catan's flexibility is part of why it's a sort of ambassador for Eurogames, a popular genre of board game built on the principle that, broadly speaking, games should be more about creating a shared experience of *play* than about the singular pursuit of victory that characterizes the classics of the American dining room table. Players in Eurogames are rarely eliminated before the end of a game the way they are in *Monopoly*; there's more strategy required to win than in the functionally random *Candyland*; and players are encouraged to focus more on trading and accumulating resources rather than crushing their opponents as in *Battleship* or *Stratego*.

Well-designed Eurogames, and *Catan* in particular, are perfect cushions for your time: complex enough that they can command the bulk of your attention, preventing you from thinking about other, less pleasant things, but not so complicated that they cause a mental short circuit. They're bearable in painful situations—this particular game of *Catan* functioned much the same way the *People* magazines did for the other women in the waiting room.

This quality also means that these games are very fun to play while drunk: my first game of *Catan* was with a few members of my college fraternity, who insisted that I would, in fact, have a good time trying to build across this abstracted, fictional island. It helped that I was not exactly sober at the time.

In getting me to hunch over the board, laid out on a dirty glass table in front of a busted pleather couch, my friends were overcoming considerable internal resistance. My first encounter with *Catan* was about two years earlier, when a pair of high school students thinking of applying to my college decided to play *Catan* on their overnight visit to campus. For some reason, they had chosen to play this weird-sounding game instead of joining me at a party in another fraternity's basement where everyone had to pay for drinks and put in a concerted effort to rip their shoes off the permanently sticky basement floor while weaving through an equally permanent haze of cigarette smoke. As an eighteen-year-old prospective philosophy major who had already planned out a senior thesis about the intersection of neo-Kantian and neo-Aristotelian ethics, it seems safe to say I was on pretty solid footing when I mocked the two teens for being nerds.

They were right to blow off the party. I don't remember much of that night in the basement, but, faded as I was, I still remember my first game of *Catan*. Or, at least, I remember how it made me feel: my initial confusion, followed by the slow sensation of starting to understand how to speak a new language, followed by the sort of pleasant frustration that comes with getting your ass kicked in an exciting new game, followed by a commitment to playing again and again until I won. When I learned about the Longest Road, a mechanic in which the player with the longest contiguous set of roads nets two victory points, I seized on it as somehow crucial to success and feverishly spent my first six or seven games trying to acquire it, to the detriment of literally every other part of the game. (It took me a while to realize an important fact that might be useful for new players: Longest Road is a tactic for fools. It can easily be disrupted or stolen by someone else, while the resource production of cities can be reinvested in development cards while making it easier to do everything else. Trust me.)

I lost that first game very badly but discovered that a fire had been lit somewhere in the lower-left part of my skull, and not just by the frat house's accordion gravity bong. I simply could not stop playing *Catan*, I told myself, at least not until I'd won a game. I stumbled around in the dark both literally and figuratively for several games, slowly trying to grasp how the rules fit together. Eventually everything started to snap into place—in a flash, the small wooden buildings that initially seemed like chunky versions of *Monopoly* houses and hotels became settlements and cities, habitation that I had carved out from the raw materials of the island and that I could then use to produce sheep, wheat, ore, lumber, and brick, which I needed to build even more settlements and cities and, after some time, to win the game. When I moved the robber piece, I wasn't just taking a card from one of the other players; I was cutting off an entire area of the island, where their villagers would otherwise be hard at work. My goal of ten, abstracted victory points was a clear horizon, but charting a straightforward course there was anything but easy. After a few weeks of failed attempts, I finally won a game. (To the best of my recollection, by *not* pursuing Longest Road.) I was hooked.

In the seemingly endless stretch of *Catan* games I played over the next two years, I would insist on everything being just right: a dim room, lit by a lantern my roommates had bought online (also while drunk); music that wasn't necessarily Howard Shore's score for the *Lord of the Rings* movies but that wasn't *not* Howard Shore's score for the *Lord of the Rings* movies; a shaky, single-game story that expanded to contain all of the quirks of resource distribution and building. (Did you build a settlement in the middle of my road, cutting off my path to build more? Think of the children!) One of the people in the fraternity moved out of the house, leaving behind a copy of the official *Settlers of Catan* novel, which he was then too embarrassed to claim. I promptly stole it and made a habit of reading a paragraph out loud in the middle of every game of *Catan* I played without knowing anything else about the plot or setting. The book, which I gathered was about a bunch of characters with names like "Candamir" and "Osmond" complaining about traveling up and down a mountain while dramatically expressing that they were also wary of witches, felt like the apotheosis of using the game to tell a story, albeit a bit too seriously.

Playing *Catan* in a darkened room under perfectly replicated conditions is a very silly habit, but it's representative of a huge piece of what draws us into board games: the story. Not the story of the game itself, necessarily—*Catan* isn't *Dungeons & Dragons*, and no one goes into a play session hoping to fall under the spell of an engrossing narrative. But you *do* participate in *making* the story every time you sit down to play the game, even if it's just the events of that individual session. Each time you prepare a game of *Monopoly*, you and everyone else in the room are consciously deciding to enter into an abstracted real estate market, where only one person will emerge victorious with all of the money. Constantly negotiating what is actually happening within the game is just one part of allowing the rules of the game to fully enmesh you; even at the same time that you put a red block on a *Catan* board, you're *also* building a settlement. It's an engrossing experience, alluding to what the pioneering cultural historian Johan Huizinga referred to as the "magic circle," a concept has been taken up by games designers and scholars for years and used to delineate the distinction between a game and the rest of one's life.

* * *

As products, board games are thriving. The amount of money Americans, in particular, spend on board games has skyrocketed in recent years, and global board game sales have started to approach $10 billion. But that doesn't mean board games are always taken seriously. No one bats an eye at books aimed at mass audiences analyzing film, television, and, increasingly, video games, but it feels absurd to imagine a newspaper hiring an in-house board game or tabletop game critic to think about the ongoing evolution of the medium. What is there to learn from the bad luck of landing in *Monopoly* jail or the zing of tweezers touching metal in *Operation* anyway? It's only so much cardboard and plastic. There's quite a lot to learn, as it turns out: board games have been used as teaching tools since their inception.

Chess, along with many other popular games, was originally a war simulation, used both as a way to spend an afternoon and as a tool for developing strategies on the battlefield. The game now commonly called *Chutes and Ladders* began its life in India over two thousand years ago as a sort of illustration of karma, with each snake and ladder representing a vice or virtue. The original *Checkered Game of Life*, the game published in 1860 by Milton Bradley that eventually became the household staple *Life*, used a similar approach to modeling right conduct, asking players to aim to land on values like perseverance and industry while avoiding the pitfalls of idleness and gambling. It was one of many successful games from the Victorian era, when publishers could begin to mass-produce their offerings—the beginning of board games as we know them today.

Most early board games were simple race games: boards where players rolled the dice and moved along a prescribed track, following orders on any given space, until they reached the end. (Many popular board games today have yet to go beyond this mechanic, or rule structure.) Passing through these scenes while subject to the whims of fate was, in theory, enough to mold young minds to any end game designers had in mind, whether civic virtue, workplace efficiency, or education about exciting new technologies. Or, at least, the world's board game manufacturers managed to convince large numbers of parents this was the case.

McLoughlin Brothers, for years one of America's biggest board game manufacturers, promised that its 1895 *Game of Mail, Express, or Accommodation* would "impart to the players a considerable amount of geographical and statistical information, and convey a vivid idea of the variety and extent of our country's productions." Manufacturer J. W. Spear & Sons' early 1900s game *International Mail: An Instructive Game* proclaimed, "the usefulness of such a game as this is obvious." McLoughlin Brothers described its *North Pole* (1897) game as the children's equivalent of a "cinematograph lecture," delivered by a real Arctic explorer. Play required moving between spaces depicting episodes of ice fishing, setting up camp, and dog sledding. How else were North American youth to learn about conditions in the tundra?

Of course, this wasn't all that early board games taught children. The cover of another McLoughlin Brothers game published around the turn of the century, *The Funny Game of Hit or Miss*, depicts a caricatured black boy with curled hair pulling away in surprise as he is whacked in the face with a ball. In the game, players spun a teetotum (a sort of top that replaced dice for gambling-averse parents) and moved across the red-and-black checkered board to see if they would "hit" or "miss." "To hit," the rules told players, "is to stop on a Negro head."

To play a board game about a given subject is to be told that it's worth spending a lot of time thinking about the topic, even if it's something as silly as anthropomorphic gumdrops. (I still remember the names of every character in *Candyland*.) For something to be the subject of a game, it must be a subject of *play*, something that can (and, at least in the eyes of the designer, should) be treated with a light touch—whether that's the candy machinations of Lord Licorice, owning *Monopoly*'s Boardwalk, or repeatedly smacking a black child in the head. Board games help define what we consider broadly acceptable, both for children who have them in the house and for hobbyist adults.

Certainly, that's been the case for most of my life. As a child in the 1990s, I played a healthy amount of family board games: *Life*, *Stratego*, the occasional game of *Scrabble*. Mostly, I used them as platforms to fantasize and daydream about other things—especially *Road to the White House*, a 1992 game that modeled the process for running a presidential campaign and included way too much paper money in the box, which I would stare at while imagining what it might be like to work in politics as an adult. I spent a lot of time looking at *Road to the White House* but very little time actually playing it. (As best I can recall, even as an eight-year-old, I had a lot of difficulty convincing my friends to play complicated board games.) Eventually, I developed cooler interests, like fantasy novels and anime, and left board games by the wayside for most of my adolescence. But once *Catan* got its hooks in me, I was a goner: by the time I graduated from college in 2014, I had returned to board games with a vengeance. I include this brief history not because I think it's especially important that I used to play *Stratego* but because the way I've been shaped by games reflects, in part, the way other people are shaped by games—and the reasons games are worth considering and reading in the first place.

* * *

A year into my *Catan* phase, large portions of my life were built around the game. I used games as an excuse to suggest plans (hey, maybe we should go on a road trip to Milwaukee?), as a setting to talk through problems in a social circle (two friends in a social group who were dating had broken up, and we needed to figure out how to make things less awkward for everyone), and even as a way of feeling out potential romantic prospects (I'm ashamed to admit this worked several times). Just before my twenty-first birthday, my then-girlfriend lured me to a surprise party with the prospect of playing *Catan*. Greeted by most of my friends, a beautiful afternoon, and a healthy selection of drinks, I deadpanned, "Does this mean we're not settling?"

Once I graduated from college, I moved from Chicago to New York, where, needing to start over with a new set of friends, I spent months futilely trying to lay the groundwork for a regular *Catan* league, complete with matching monogrammed bowling shirts. This would, in theory, be a regularly structured, regimented way of interacting with other people and forming long-term social bonds (read: avoiding loneliness in a newish city). It didn't work, but I *did* cement a few friendships by playing one-off games. *Catan*'s game pieces became a cardboard foundation for my relationships, and I was not alone.

As it is for many enthusiasts, *Catan* was my on-ramp for modern hobby board games—the sort that most people tend to think of as overly complex, confusing, and in the province of nerds. (Many hobby games are Eurogames, but not all. "Hobby games" refers to games played primarily by adults who devote their time to gaming as a hobby, rather than any particular genre or rule set. Hobby games are, in turn, just one segment of tabletop games: all games that one traditionally plays on a table with physical components, whether that involves a board, cards, or other items.) As a relatively easy-to-play game that still *sounds* ridiculously complicated, *Catan* has often served as a stand-in for the larger popularity of those games. In a 2013 episode of *Parks & Recreation*, Adam Scott's nerdy character, Ben Wyatt, insists on playing *Catan* at his bachelor party. (Mayfair, the company that publishes *Catan*, built a board for *The Cones of Dunshire*, the intentionally convoluted and obtuse game Ben creates in a later episode.) A crowd-funded short film called *Lord of Catan* depicts the breakdown of a couple's marriage, played by nerd-favorite actors Fran Kranz and Amy Acker. *Catan* has appeared multiple times on *The Big Bang Theory*.

Catan is so popular that it's even spilled over into areas of culture where you wouldn't expect to find board games. In 2012, the Green Bay Packers football team, led by its offensive line, became deadly serious about *Catan*. After players started to talk about the team's love of *Catan* on sports radio, football fans in Wisconsin flooded hobby stores demanding copies of the game. Eventually, the *Wall Street Journal* published a profile about the team's *Catan* habit—games were so competitive that when a player left the room to finish grilling dinner for the other players, he refused to accept the eventual result of the game. (He did not win.)

As a piece of culture, *Catan* is essentially a cross-over hit, finding purchase with audiences possessing different levels of board game experience and expertise like a massively popular space-opera film or highly specific house song that finds mainstream success. Its flexibility and complexity separate *Catan* from most American family games, which tend to take the form of chance-based races, miniature tactical simulations, and trivia contests. In this case, *Catan*'s crossover potential operates within any given game session. When you sit down to play, you might bridge the gap between different gaming communities and possibly even between dissimilar members of your family, actively inviting the two or three other players to join you in the magic circle.

Though the concept had been floating around for some time, designers Eric Zimmerman and Katie Salen took up the "magic circle" in their 2003 book *Rules of Play*, where it is broadly used to delineate between a game and the rest of life. But after years of debate, Zimmerman had to clarify his meaning and take the concept of the magic circle down a peg in a 2012 online essay about a fictional "magic circle jerk." (Apparently a person enamored with the structural implications of the magic circle and not a euphemism for an academic conference.) Here, Zimmerman condenses the useful part of what to understand about the magic circle as a lens for thinking about games: "when a game is being played, new meanings are generated." The magic circle is the boundary within which everyone's behavior becomes, if not governed by the rules of whatever game everyone has agreed to play, then at least influenced by it—within the magic circle, you aren't just your *D&D* character or Colonel Mustard, you're also trying to think the way the game wants you to think, to act the way the game wants you to act.

But of course, there isn't a one-to-one correlation between game rules and how they influence players. Unlike a video game that frequently has a set way for you to play through it and lives as code, board games require other people, and they only exist when you choose to play them. Games take on different characters in different contexts, with the same set of rules conforming themselves to a smoky party or a family dining room. This power that a board game has—the way it invites you to interact with it, to become what it wants you to become—is the central thing I'm interested in when I play games and when I think about them. It's the main thing I want to explore here. And, obviously, it's why my family loves *Catan*.

* * *

In January 2016, after much prompting on my end, my brother, sister, and I played our first game of *Catan* together. My initial *Catan* obsession had cooled a bit, but I really wanted to find a game to play with them. The three of us had just become adult siblings—one day we struggled to find things to talk about, the next our relationships became comfortable and close in a way that has barely changed since. (I'm technically an adult man, but I spend a lot of time hiding with my sister in her room talking about *Charmed* when we're supposed to be downstairs mingling at family events.) More accessible than most of the other games I was into at the time, *Catan* was a natural choice; it helped that, as a seasoned veteran, I steamrolled everyone in our first game. Or, at least, that's my recollection. My sister claims she actually won our first game—but whom are you going to believe?

We became obsessed with *Catan*, playing it any time all three of us were in the same place. At first, our parents were excited that the three of us were spending so much time together, but as our dedication to fitting in more and more games grew (our record is five in a day, fifteen in a weekend), our mother began to greet the sight of the board with an exasperated sigh. And it didn't help that my sister was in high school and ostensibly should have been doing her homework or something. It didn't matter. As our competition intensified, there was nothing anyone could do to stop it. All three of us independently downloaded the *Catan* mobile app and played obsessively against the game's AI (with the same vaguely Germanic names as the characters from the novel), trying to hone our skills to the point where we'd be primed and ready to strike at a moment's notice. We've refused to leave the kitchen for the better part of a day. We've sneaked away on family vacations, ignoring scheduled activities in order to play with a little plastic travel set. We now have a running spreadsheet tracking who has won each game and with what number of victory points—and though we have yet to produce any significant findings from these games, the important thing is having all of the data, just in case.

I won most of our earlier, prespreadsheet games. Now my brother, who is much more tactically minded than I am, takes home most of the victories. Still, part of the reason we keep playing is that anybody could win any given game. *Catan* can be complex enough to encourage quantitative gamers—for example, my brother, who studied economics in college and is by far the most consistent competitor in our family. But it can be calm enough to encourage healthy table talk and to allow players to come from behind and win suddenly—for example, my sister, who frequently wins games after seeming to be far behind the rest of us. And it can allow you to be socially devious, to win by getting under the skin of other players—for example, me. If you ask my brother and sister, they'll say I often complain about being targeted in a game and incessantly try to convince them that I'm losing, only to sneak ahead and win the game in the last stretch. I have no idea how I got this reputation.

Catan's success is partly about the mechanics, but it's also about the story and setting: the narrative you're creating every time you sit down to play. What is *Catan* actually about? What story were my brother, sister, and I telling five times in one day, besides the story that, as my sister likes to remind us, "Sammy is the best at everything"? Three or four fledgling empires expand across the pristine, newfound island of Catan, competing to establish themselves as the first to claim dominance. That description doesn't do justice to why *Catan* is compelling, but I think that's part of the point: a game becomes compelling because the *players* make it that way. In this case, the skeleton of the *Catan* rules is just strong enough for any given game to hold whatever the players hang onto it.

The power of that narrative comes from the players, but it also comes from *Catan*'s creator, the German game designer Klaus Teuber. A former dental technician, Teuber had originally planned a series of several games exploring early colonization on a grand time line before scrapping the expansive, sprawling project and condensing everything down into *Catan*'s smooth, streamlined engine. Teuber's lifelong love of Viking civilization influenced not just the initial incarnation of *Catan* but also the entire conglomerate that *Catan* has evolved into—the merchandise, the tournaments, and even the book. (Rebecca Gable, the writer of the *Catan* novel, is a historical novelist by trade.)

In practice, the most visible vestige of *Catan*'s origins—and the one that players are most likely to interact with and be influenced by—is the robber, the only native of Catan to appear in the game and the only actual character not under the control of the players. When someone rolls a seven or plays a knight card, they get to move the robber (which blocks off a new space on the board) and take a resource card from another player. Originally a piece of black wood, the piece was eventually changed into a nondescript gray blob, more of a placeholder for the robber of your imagination than anything else.

In Teuber's telling, as laid out in a blog post on the official *Catan* website, that blob is actually three separate people: a group of hapless bandits who are forced to move between the different hexagons by the players in an existentially agonizing, unending series of involuntary migrations. This is the story *Catan* tells itself and one that, apparently, is supposed to be funny. It's a story that, unsurprisingly, has a lot in common with the story of colonization—people in power telling themselves that their actions don't have *real* consequences, because everything they're doing is a sort of game affecting people who aren't really people, only pawns. What other way is there to win?

At 2014's GenCon, North America's largest tabletop-gaming convention, the game designer Bruno Faidutti gave a largely improvised, tongue-in-cheek lecture titled "Postcolonial Catan," holding a funhouse mirror up to the game's narrative. Taking this apparently frivolous idea—that *Catan*'s abstracted island plays out the narrative of colonialism—Faidutti drew on his own history in the industry, a healthy sense of humor, and Edward Said's classic work *Orientalism*, which analyzes the history of Western depictions of colonized peoples, to diagnose a chronic condition in board game design, perhaps produced by an emphasis on the mechanics and rules needed to balance the way players act on a game, rather than the ways the game acts on the players. In the lecture (later transformed into a mildly inflammatory online essay), Faidutti asks gamers to consider another thing that is, ostensibly, happening on the board: the natives of Catan are being steamrolled.

Catan is participating in a common gaming narrative. The "age of exploration" readily lends itself to common ways of thinking about games, positing the player as general or king of an army of forces totally at their control—an approach brought over from classic war-gaming, a genre in which the point of the game isn't to have fun or engage in play as much as it is to accurately reproduce the conditions of a historical battle. (The most complex war games frequently attempt to capture details ranging from the altitude of specific terrain to the foods soldiers ate to the make and model of their guns.) But this goes beyond the European colonization period—other games use the iconography of ancient Egypt, Edo-era Japan, and even Hawaiian civilization to add "color" (both literally and figuratively) to a game, even when it has nothing to do with what the game is actually about. In other words, you could create a few abstract game rules, spin a wheel of lazy settings, and start selling your product.

As I've become more interested in games and learned more about their history, I've gotten the sense that debates within the community tend to take on the same character over and over again. Many longtime gamers get into the hobby because they respond to the system of a game—the way the rules structure your interactions with other people, the way they encourage you to marvel at the feat of mathematical construction, and, often, the way they replicate previously existing things like a battle or a particular sort of market. On the other hand, newer players and those less embedded in the hobby frequently respond to novelty, largely in the form of narrative—and, accordingly, everything from the introduction of *Magic: The Gathering* to *Dungeons & Dragons* has caused loud debates among game designers and enthusiasts.

For years, these debates caused tension within gaming, only for the upstart to rapidly become assimilated into the establishment. An essay by the designer Rick Loomis, published in a 2000 anthology titled *Horsemen of the Apocalypse*, tracked several cycles' worth of conflict in an attempt to identify the phenomenon; apparently early arguments were so intense that war-gamers used to derisively refer to board gamers as "cardboard pushers" who were "debasing the hobby." The same thing played out again with the introduction of fantasy role-playing, prompting many board gamers to show up at conventions wearing shirts with slogans attacking *Dun-*

geons & Dragons. Eventually, *everybody* teamed up on the newfound success of *Magic*, which had the gall to be a *card* game.

I bring this up mostly to set up the day when, half asleep and trying to fit my mouth around an entire mug of coffee, I listened to Faidutti discussing "postcolonial *Catan*" in conversation with one of the hosts of the popular board game podcast *Ludology*. Though the host made an effort to engage with what Faidutti was saying, I almost spit out my coffee in shock that he had never really even considered the idea that colonialism—or, less academically, centuries of human suffering—was an ever-present part of the foundations of the games he designed and played and that he had never really considered the possibility that it might be a good idea to try to interrogate why that was and how it could be fixed. You can't really blame gamers for, as the host put it, "not wanting to think about subjugating people to score points." But then again, neither did the people doing the initial subjugation. Some gamers do not have the opportunity to ignore what the host referred to as "the native issue."

* * *

What would it look like to tell a healthier story, to understand how fundamental these tropes are to board games and push back against them? In 2017, Greater Than Games published the designer R. Eric Reuss's *Spirit Island*, an attempt at a colonial revenge fantasy in which players take on the roles of the nature spirits on a mostly pristine island. Invaders—colonial powers, pointedly represented by white plastic conquistador figurines—have attempted to take over the island, stripping the land for resources and blighting it in the process, unsettling the natural harmony. You, the spirits, have to wipe them out while working together with the native humans to protect the island from further damage.

In creating *Spirit Island*, Reuss was responding to and attempting to "reverse" the trend of strategy games that uncritically posit players as colonizing forces leading European fleets. In one section of the rule book, Reuss writes, "I wonder how ticked off the locals are about this new colony of foreigners. Well, we'll never know because this game has *entirely abstracted away* the people who already lived there. *That's* rude." Putting aside the effect of referring to colonization as "rude," it's a noble impulse and one that wound up being highly rewarding in game form.

While Reuss cites several other Eurogames as partial inspirations for *Spirit Island*, it's impossible not to look at the board—a seemingly untouched island divided into several types of territories, bordered by ocean—the cities and towns that make up the invaders' homes, and the box's description of the game as a "settler destruction strategy game" and not see it as, at least in part, responding to *Catan*. Depending on how you pronounce it, "Dahan," the name for the native people of the island, sounds awfully like "Catan." Reuss claims this was a coincidence, but that doesn't really matter. It's still there for the players, if they want to find it.

Spirit Island is a cooperative game, which means the players aren't competing against each other. Instead, a deck of cards sets the invaders' actions in motion, and you win or lose as a group. (More on this later.) This change alters the character of play enormously, leading interaction with the rules to mostly take the form of collective conversations about the best way to push back against them—how to stop the invaders from building a new city, how to make sure they don't ravage the island's wetlands, how to strike enough fear into their hearts that they'll turn and flee.

Catan is the type of game that appears complicated at first but quickly reveals itself to be relatively simple. *Spirit Island* is . . . a little more intense. Like an arcane war game re-creating D-Day, there are all sorts of hidden or nested rules that pop up to ruin your game just when you think you're on top of the settlers. I didn't even finish playing my first game with some of the members of a weekly board game group I frequented in March 2018—partly because we foolishly and arrogantly thought we could learn how to play at a bar and partly because the spiraling nature of the invaders' attempts at conquering the island made it almost impossible for us to understand what was going on. After two or three turns, we packed the box away, and I took it home in shame. Eventually, two of my roommates and I began playing semifrequently, at least once or twice a week, until we started to get a better handle on the rules and how to work together to subvert them.

According to the background in *Spirit Island*'s rule book, the Dahan were originally at odds with the spirits, eventually forming a literal contract to make sure that both parties were capable of living at peace—the sin of the invaders is not that they wanted to take the land, but that they didn't sign anything before doing so. This, in a sense, mirrors the arrangement that establishes the pretext for any shared game experience, in which all players decide on what they're about to do and enter into a sort of loose pact to obey the rules. When my siblings sit down to play a game of *Catan*, we're all in rough agreement about what it is we're going to do.

Still, for all of the evident care Reuss has taken to try to make the island feel like its own, original creation without appropriating or aping a preexisting culture or colonial struggle in the manner of the games Faidutti criticizes, the end result is a little toothless. It's harder to get a sense of what might be at stake if the people you're defending never existed in the first place, to say nothing of the magical spirits that (probably) didn't exist. At the end of the rule book section that finishes laying out all of the actual rules needed to play *Spirit Island*, Reuss dramatically asks, "Can you save the island?"—a question that invites you to ask what happens when the island *isn't* saved. The answer is something very similar to our own world, where colonial invaders *did* succeed at mostly wiping out and subduing native populations. We're already living in *Spirit Island*'s worst-case scenario, and part of what the game provides is the opportunity to methodically act out a fantasy of things going differently.

* * *

Whether it's *Catan*, *Spirit Island*, or *The Funny Game of Hit and Miss*, board games communicate ideas, just like any other piece of culture. And though board games are more popular than they have been in decades, the tools to think about the ideas they contain are unevenly distributed—the relatively closed-off world of academic game studies here, a review site or two there, largely operating from within the hobbyist perspective (i.e., people who are interested in and know a lot about board games talking to other people who are interested in and know a lot about board games). These types of conversations are absolutely important, and I've learned a lot from them. But criticism proves valuable in a number of different ways, and one of them is reaching laypeople, both as an act of recommendation (what should I buy?) and a way of getting them to think about art—and their own lives—in a different way. We're a ways away from having the tools to think and write that way about board games, to listen to them on a broader scale.

A game like *Spirit Island* doesn't exactly speak to you—not directly, at least. The whole point of the medium is the way it sneaks into your play experience, the way that there isn't really a game when you're not playing, at least not in the same way there's a film when you're not watching it or an album when you're not listening to it. Instead, there's the space that's created by the rules and by the agreement everyone has made to abide by them, whether that's happening at a party, in a sticky living room, or on a dining room table. Board games are systems, scaffolds that we hang our experiences on, crucibles that form moments like sitting in a hospital waiting room, half watching *Vanderpump Rules*, running out the clock.

About two-thirds of the way through that game in the hospital, our parents came over and tapped us on the shoulder, signaling that it was time to go to our grandfather's hospital room. I'm not especially interested in talking about what happened in the room, other than to say that it was a numbing experience, of the sort that is so vivid you can remember all of the small details any time you try to remember it, even if you don't want to. But once we'd finished our too-brief moment of saying good-bye, our family went back to the waiting room. Everything was the same, everything was a little different. My brother, sister, and I sat down, looked at each other for a moment, and, without a word, started rolling the dice.

2

PLAYING ALONG WITH COMPLICITY

For the first time, my Brooklyn basement was packed full of Jews hungry for Shabbat dinner. Ten or so people had come over to eat falafel out of plastic dishes, drink kiddush wine from a glass I'd borrowed from my parents, and wear yarmulkes I'd bought at a nearby Judaica store. But they'd also come over on that misty, brisk night in February to play *Juden Raus*, a Nazi Germany–era game about forcibly removing Jewish families from their homes in order to deport them to Palestine.

After saying the necessary blessings and tucking into the food, a few of us moved over to a coffee table in a corner of the basement where I'd set up the makeshift *Juden Raus* board, printed out on a large piece of poster paper. Our version of the rules had been loosely translated from the original German by a friend and read off my phone. We used pieces from other games, since I didn't have the original wooden pieces depicting German police officers, and I *definitely* didn't have the wooden hat pieces that represented the Jewish families we'd be deporting, each one marked with a face sporting a grossly anti-Semitic scowl.

Still, I was excited: I'd been looking forward to playing *Juden Raus*. I spent weeks casually mentioning my plans to "play a Nazi board game" in conversation; most of the time, I could sense the other person starting to sprint away, even if the conversation was happening over the phone. Thankfully, I had enough friends who were morbidly curious (or at least willing to humor me) to set up a Shabbat-dinner session of *Juden Raus*. This admittedly bizarre experience was also the culmination of a years-long desire: discovering the existence of *Juden Raus* was what got me interested in the ideological uses of board games in the first place.

In the fall of 2013, at the height of my *Catan* obsession, I was enrolled in a class called New and Emerging Genres, which covered recently developed forms of storytelling like video games, interactive fiction, and autobiographical comics. Students were asked to write blog posts either responding to something someone had said in class or describing a genre we hadn't covered but that could have been included in the syllabus—why we found it compelling, what it might be able to do that other genres couldn't, and what we might have discussed were it to be the subject of a lesson. One night, looking for something new to write about and hopped up on, among other things, *Catan* and cheap beer, I stumbled upon a Wikipedia page titled "Nazi Board Games." Shocked, scintillated, and stoned in equal measure, I eagerly read up on the history of these games—specifically, on the history of *Juden Raus.*

Here's what I learned about *Juden Raus*: The game was created by Günther & Co., a game manufacturer based in the German toy hub of Dresden, as a way of cashing in on the popularity of the Nazi government's anti-Semitic policies. It was most likely published in 1936, a year after the passage of the Nuremberg Laws limited the political rights of German Jews and just two years before Kristallnacht, the pogrom that broadly initiated the Nazi government's support for mass violence against Jews. That first night, I assumed that *Juden Raus* was officially sanctioned—and possibly produced by—the Nazis. It was easy for my couch-ridden self to imagine Aryan children eagerly playing the game while sitting around the dinner table, shrieking in delight at the prospect of exiling the Jews. In fact, while I was writing my blog post, I distinctly remembered reading that Joseph Goebbels himself endorsed the game and had a hand in planning what were essentially interactive toys for Hitler Youth.

This was, it turned out, not at all correct. (Who knew there was a problem with doing research stoned? Or with relying on Wikipedia?) The page for "Nazi Board Games," or at least the version of it I looked at that night, merely cited Goebbels's principles of propaganda in relation to the existence of the game, rather than crediting him directly—and, in fact, *Juden Raus* was, to put it lightly, not a hit with the regime: in 1938, *Das Schwarze Korps*, the official newspaper of the SS, published an anonymous editorial criticizing *Juden Raus* for trivializing and profiting off the gravely important work the SS was doing to "fend off the Jewish rabble of murderers."

The rest of *Juden Raus*'s history is otherwise shrouded in mystery, up to and including how well the game actually sold. While *Juden Raus* is commonly cited as having sold about a million copies, other sources suggest that in fact it sold very poorly in the face of official opposition, and that the high initial estimates were the result of bluffing on the part of the distributor. There's some debate over the exact identity of the manufacturer, the background of the distributor, and even the year the game was published. (1936 seems most likely, but there's a chance it might have been 1938.) One rumor about the game suggested *Juden Raus* might never have actually made it to market and that the two known copies in existence were just prototypes for the never-completed final product.

At the time, I didn't know any of this information. Knowing it now, it doesn't affect the way I think about *Juden Raus*, really; the mere existence of a game about rounding up and deporting Jewish people that was actually manufactured in whatever capacity was horrifying enough to capture my imagination—the image of that Aryan family having a pleasant evening at the dining room table was simply too powerful to ignore. Apparently, the thought held a certain undeniable attraction, or perhaps compulsion, for other people as well: by the time I learned of its existence, *Juden Raus* had become something of a minor legend in the board game community. It is commonly referred to as "history's most infamous board game."

Once I learned about the *Das Schwarze Korps* editorial, it became the most fascinating part of the story. The Nazis were no strangers to spectacle: their propaganda efforts included rallies, films like *The Triumph of the Will*, and the 1936 Olympics in Berlin. Board games, apparently, crossed the line—even though, depending on what version of the history you believe, *Juden Raus* seemed to be having at least some success in winning over children to the grim, horrifying cause. If you're trying to marshal support for mass deportation and genocide, why be bashful about marketing your plan to children by whatever means you had available to you? What is it about board games that made them trivial, in contrast to any other form of Nazi hagiography? I wanted to understand what made board games special or, rather, what made them seem *not* special to most people who encountered them.

In my class blog post, I wrote that, as horrifying as *Juden Raus* was, it wasn't all that different from games that served to impart current American ideology to children. The communicative force of board games, I wrote, came from forcing the players to act out life in the system modeled by the game—and I was onto something. A board game is, effectively, a set of rules you're asked to interact with over and over in the hope of attaining some kind of fulfillment. If that sounds familiar, it might be because that's the premise behind many, many aspects of modern life that have been transformed into games: people learn languages by playing with apps like Duolingo, measure their physical activity with tools like Fitbits, and trawl for likes, favorites, and retweets on social media. Pickup-artist culture is quite literally premised on the idea of scoring. Other mundane activities—buying health insurance, visiting the DMV—are just deeply unfun games without the chance to quit. These are all games that permeate our day-to-day experience, systems of rules that we're trained to interact with in the same way we learn to play *Life*.

"Game" is frequently used as an example of a word that captures the slipperiness at the heart of living in the world and of trying to use language in it. The philosopher Ludwig Wittgenstein uses the term "language-game" to describe a particular sort of interaction one can have while using words and the rough set of rules or norms that govern those interactions. (For example, making a joke, telling a story, asking for a favor.) Many people who follow Wittgenstein's lead accordingly use "game" as an example of the way most words don't have fixed definitions, at least not in a way that supersedes how the word is actually used. Anyone attempting to identify a single characteristic that unifies and is present in all games will be disappointed. There are games where the object is not to compete with other people, games where there is no winner, and even, sometimes, games where there are no rules. "Game" as a concept refers instead to a cluster, a constellation of ideas and features. Capture the flag can be a game, but so can spin the bottle or *Halo*. All instances of games don't need to share every aspect of the definition. Games are many things, and they are—or can be—powerful.

To be fair, there are games that have next to zero influence on the people playing them—and, of course, there are people who don't take much away from the games that they play. But that's true of any form of human expression, even the ones that we spend lifetimes theorizing. The special thing about games, and tabletop games in particular, is the way they actively train you to think from within their rules. Other forms of art do this too, but in a more roundabout way that requires a certain sensitivity and willingness to be taken in by the television show you're watching or the book you're reading. With games, it's a prerequisite to entry. If you don't think the way the game wants you to think at least a little bit, you're not really playing the game at all.

Do you need to convince the other people sitting around the *Catan* board to give you their sheep, by any means necessary? Is it important to be the sole property owner at the end of a game of *Monopoly*? Is confirming the identities of possible suspects in a game of *Clue* necessary? The answer to these questions is "yes, if you are playing the game properly." In order to genuinely be playing the game, or at least playing it with enough enthusiasm and commitment that other players will recognize that you are playing, you must allow yourself to be directed by the game. Over the course of play sessions, those rules will have shaped the way you act, if only for a few brief moments, and even if that game is *Juden Raus*.

After writing my college blog post, I spent five years imagining what it would look like to actually play *Juden Raus*. Even though I probably could have thrown something together, I, too, lacked the imagination to envision what it would look like to set up a play session for the game—or, rather, I lacked the drive and internal motivation to say, "Yes, I *do* want to invest the time and energy into figuring out how to play this old Nazi board game." I did spend a lot of time thinking about it, though: when my college Birthright trip made a stop at Yad Vashem, the Israeli museum commemorating the history and legacy of the Holocaust, I asked to see its copy of *Juden Raus*, one of the two still in existence. The people at the museum did not want to take the time to show a random twenty-year-old the game board, but they had another relevant game on public display. This one was a variant on *Monopoly* created by a graphic designer in a Polish ghetto, using the properties and chance cards as a way of teaching children tools for survival. Board games, I learned, could help lead people into evil situations—but they could also be used to teach people how to escape.

* * *

The German toy and game industry has long been a crucial part of the country's manufacturing sector, based out of Dresden and Nuremberg. Air attacks destroyed several factories during World War II, but the industry bounced back and eventually became a staple of the nation's entertainment: the winner of the prestigious Spiele des Jahres prize generally sees a sales boost of several hundred thousand games, and in Germany, board games are often consciously positioned as alternatives to television or other forms of mass media. Klaus Teuber, the inventor of *Catan*, claims he began designing board games as a way to find other activities to do with his family, a motive that's been echoed by the designers of other Eurogames. The mere fact that he is a celebrity at all is a testament to the strength of German gaming culture.

Material conditions in postwar Germany also contributed to the growth of Eurogames—local companies didn't have the rights to any of the Western family games that were massively popular at the time, forcing them to make their own products. In the process, Eurogame designers worked to fix many of the problems with those same games. Playing a game with your family is no fun if your parents, siblings, or children are constantly being eliminated from play; Eurogames almost always ensure that everyone plays until the end of the game. If your family is playing a simple race game, you won't actually have in-game reasons to interact with the other people in your family, and you'll only be playing *with* them in the loosest possible sense; Eurogames frequently force players to trade resources or otherwise collaborate in order to get an advantage in the game. The winner-take-all structure of games like *Monopoly* is a big part of why they tend to be so contentious; Eurogames make it possible for even players in dire circumstances to come from behind and win.

German game designers also had another reason they needed to focus on original games: postwar German laws banned the importing of war-related toys, as well as the display of Nazi symbols outside of artistic or educational contexts. This limitation ruled out many tactical games, or attempts to simulate historical battles, excising war from German culture to the point where an article from the late 1980s describes American-style war games as being kept hidden under the table of one company's booth at the German board game convention Essen Spiel, treated as if they were illicit magazines. War simulations have a long history dating all the way back to chess, including an enormously popular German military exercise called *Kriegspiel* (literally "war game"). That tradition was essentially cut off, forcing Eurogame inventors to prioritize different design principles, modeling different forms of competition. This meant asking players to engage in activities like trading, negotiating, and managing resources rather than combat. It also meant heavily abstracting games, removing the thematic specificity required for most war games.

Meanwhile, Americans with the leisure time needed to craft full simulations of Napoleonic battles were instrumental in the emergence of other, more complicated types of battle simulation. A decent chunk of American national self-image is still shaped by the narrative of World War II: the entire *Indiana Jones* series rests on the premise that destroying people's sacred landmarks is totally fine as long as you're defending them from *Nazis*. War movies will continue to win Academy Awards as long as they continue to make Academy voters feel good about themselves. And games like the *Axis & Allies* tabletop series and *Call of Duty* video game franchise rest on endlessly replicating the war. Eventually, American war-game designers moved into replicating the conditions of medieval battles, a development that helped lead to the emergence of *Dungeons & Dragons* and thereby modern role-playing games.

Any cultural form grows around its limitations. The act structure of a TV episode accommodates commercial breaks, and studio romantic comedies wrapped around Hollywood's Production Code. Eventually, art forms consume themselves, commenting on the conditions of their creation. The experimental use of the Holocaust and World War II as inspiration and subject matter has found its apotheosis in the American game designer Brenda Romero's *Train*. This game was designed for her series *The Mechanic Is the Message*, a group of games exploring the use of mechanics (essentially, rules and structures that make up the game) as a way to communicate—or inflict—serious emotional response. In this case, the stated subject of *Train* is "complicity." Romero sets out to interrogate what people will and won't do in the process of playing a game and obeying the rules, what another person might call "following orders."

Imagine that you are playing a game of *Train*. You will be asked to complete a simple challenge: fitting yellow pawns depicting people into a train car, then moving the car along a track sitting on top of the pane of glass. You'll read the rules off a page inserted into an actual typewriter near the board. These rules are, however, intentionally incomplete, so you and the rest of your group will be forced to agree on how to proceed, filling in gaps in the rules and acting as partial designers of the game you'll be playing. In any given session of *Train*, you have consciously committed to what you understand play to be and, eventually, to the consequences of that play.

There are several clues to the real subject of the game, including a key on the typewriter emblazoned with the SS's logo and breaks in the glass, intended to evoke Kristallnacht, but if you have not noticed these components throughout the game, you will eventually flip over a card that reveals that the train you are packing has, in fact, gone to Auschwitz. The yellow pawns represent the six million Jews killed in the Holocaust, and the number and color of the pieces drives home the scope of what you are being asked to do, what you have in fact done. Your game of *Train* for all intents and purposes ends when you discover this information, and the endgame takes the form of your reaction. How you feel when you learn what is happening in *Train*, how you feel having done something that you didn't actually do but obviously still *did*, is the whole point of the game.

Many of the people who have played *Train* cried at the end. Some became angry at Romero for tricking them into having a gameplay experience in which they felt they had contributed to an atrocity. Several committed to undermining the narrative of the game in some way, usually by hiding the pawns underneath the train car or trying to take them out of the play space. None of these is a definitive or "correct" reaction to *Train*, in the same way that there isn't a definitive or "correct" reaction to a provocative, powerful work of art or in the same way that there isn't one definitive or "correct" way to exist in a world where you passively participate in innumerable systems of violence and horror simply by being alive. The haphazard and experimental nature of the end of *Train* may lead one to ask whether it is even a game at all, a question that, no matter how you answer it, doesn't matter nearly as much as what *Train* suggests about what games can be.

Romero was inspired to begin her *The Mechanic Is the Message* series when her young daughter came home from school and attempted to explain what she'd learned about the Middle Passage, in terms that suggested she thought that, in Romero's words, "some black people went on a cruise." Using an impromptu setup to represent the horrible conditions of slave ships, Romero had her daughter paint pieces to create several families, then separated many of them between "land" and the boat, where gameplay took place. Eventually, they had to decide whether to throw people off the boat or off the boat or risk mass starvation and illness. Romero had successfully imparted the spark of horror and understanding to her daughter—she had begun to grasp the scope of what had happened and what it might be like to experience a similar ordeal.

The New World, as the game became known, was the first in the series. Other installments track the history of Romero's Irish ancestors, the economics of illegal immigration and food's importance in Mexican culture, and the Trail of Tears. (This last one has fifty thousand pieces.) Over the past few years, the aims of the series seem to have come into focus as central to whatever ongoing cultural project we want games to be engaged in. When elected officials ask for "thoughts and prayers" as a way of preventing school shootings, they're called "complicit" in the eventual atrocities. When celebrities remain silent, they are criticized and called complicit for their refusal to speak up about ongoing injustice. In each case, the complicit party is accused of complicity precisely because they are part of a system that reproduces injustice—the entertainment industry, the government, gun violence—and choose not to push back against the rules of that system. They are the victorious players.

When this idea is taken to its natural conclusion, however, it's hard to avoid the thought that everyone is, more or less, complicit in everything. That's the nature of living at the crossroads created by all of the different systems that shape our experience. We call for better conditions for workers while buying things on Amazon because it's convenient. We criticize studios and record labels for promoting art made by monstrous people, while secretly watching Woody Allen movies or listening to Kanye. We know that gig workers are being exploited by tech companies but continue to take Ubers and Lyfts precisely *because* they're so cheap and easy. Or, at least, I do. (Not you, though. *You* have definitely never compromised with the world, not once.) As much as we would like to think we would refuse to sign the contract that *Train* asks us to formalize, for most of us, it's already happened.

Being a better person, being a better player, and whatever it looks like to navigate the tension between the two requires acknowledging that you are already playing from within a system and figuring out what it would look like to engage in the equivalent of hiding the pieces under the train. Systems, whether they're explicitly presented in the form of games or not, dictate and shape our lives, like water being held in an awkwardly shaped vase. Maintaining a sense of frustration and anger at the shape forced on your existence, and that of countless others, is of the utmost necessity for a politically productive life. This uncomfortable awareness was what I intended to replicate with my rainy-day *Juden Raus* session.

* * *

Juden Raus is, ultimately, a pretty simple game. The board depicts a walled German city (likely Berlin) crisscrossed by roads and spaces representing the homes of Jewish families. The player pieces, designed to resemble German police officers, move through the city, collecting a "hat" piece with a grotesque caricature of a Jew each time they land on one of the homes. (This component of the game is based on *Fang den Hut*, a German game whose title translates as "capture the hat," in turn derived from the same Indian folk game that eventually became *Parcheesi*.) Players must then return to their "collection point," where they can drop off the Jew piece and head back into the city. The first player to bring six Jews to their designated "collection point" wins the game. The text on the board roughly translates to "Display skill in the game, so that you collect many Jews!"; "When you drive out six Jews, you will be the winner without question!"; and "Off to Palestine!" It's quite the exodus.

Going into the session, I'd expected to be able to get started with the game pretty quickly, since the rules seemed so simple. I was wrong—there were questions about whether or not the Jewish families replenished in their spaces each time a player kidnapped one of them, whether you could have two families at once in your possession, and when, if ever, players had the opportunity to choose which direction they moved in rather than simply heading toward the center of town, which operated as the drop-off point and main hub for the game. These were gaps in the rules that needed to be filled, creating an ad hoc implicit contract over the course of play like the one in *Train*. Even if the game we played was not the textbook version of *Juden Raus* played by little Aryan children in the 1930s, it didn't matter; we'd agreed on what it was we were doing and consciously chose to follow those rules to their logical, grim conclusion. It was an agreement that *this* was how we were going to play the game about Nazi deportation of Jewish families.

Most of my other expectations for the *Juden Raus* session were upended. I had anticipated that one or more of my friends would become visibly upset while we were playing—though all of us had had our fair share of experiences with unpleasant play (and all of us were effectively desensitized to violence after long lives of twenty-first-century media consumption), being asked to explicitly participate in the literal Holocaust might, perhaps, be a pill a bit too bitter for everyone to swallow. And indeed, even I, the organizer of the session and the person who wanted to play *Juden Raus* in the first place, was a bit overcome at the beginning of the game as I picked up my first token, repurposed to represent a Jewish family I'd dragged from their home and brought back to a government collection point. It was the first time I'd responded so viscerally to a tabletop game in years. I'd blocked out some time at the end of the games for us to discuss what it was like to play and possibly to work through our shared discomfort together. But more than anything, it turned out that playing *Juden Raus* was *boring*.

In theory, we should have been horrified by rolling dice to participate in organized violence against Jews. But the race-game component of *Juden Raus* won out over the race game component: no amount of thematic excitement or revulsion can make up for the fact that the players aren't actually being asked to *do* much of anything besides rolling dice. At the beginning of the game, we cut the tension with nervous laughter, tentatively navigating the rules as we started to settle on what it would look like for us to play *Juden Raus*, partly as a way of relieving anxiety but also as a way of protecting ourselves from the effects of the game. But by the time a rhythm set in, we were totally inured to *Juden Raus* and to the thing we'd been trying to navigate around in the first place.

Eventually, *Juden Raus* was overtaken by other things—tableside conversation about our lives, our work, who we were dating—just like an ordinary board game session around an ordinary dining room table. After a while, the game of *Juden Raus* transformed into an extended wait to see who would win, and my basement felt filled with the thick air of a poorly taught and poorly ventilated high school science class. Rather than disgusted, I just felt numb. About an hour later, struggling to finish a couple of bottles of red wine and discussing our gameplay experience, someone suggested that *Juden Raus* was probably a failure as an attempt at propaganda: it wasn't an interesting enough game to capture our attention, so it probably wouldn't have been as captivating for children who could just as easily have been indoctrinated into Nazi ideology by their parents, schools, and the news. *Juden Raus*, on this reading, was more of a curiosity than anything else.

This understanding of the game certainly lines up with most people's experience playing didactic, educational games—they tend to be intolerably boring and often inspire instinctive, aggressive resistance from young players. These games frequently fail at communicating the message they're designed to convey or are reduced to operating under the radar. But, tipsy, reflexively contrarian (and interested in defending my expertise and understanding of how the game worked), I claimed that it might have actually been the opposite. The boring miasma of a race game makes it easier to accept what you're doing as ordinary, since there's nothing less pressing or morally compelling than being bored. Wasn't it possible, I suggested, that families playing *Juden Raus* were actually led to think of deporting Jews as *precisely* a mundane activity, undeserving of scrutiny and officially sanctioned so that it eventually becomes an accepted part of life? By the end of the second game, one of my friends cheered each time she successfully brought a family back to the collection point.

Looking into the history of tabletop games, it's not so hard to encounter the seductive power of being asked to inhabit the Nazi position. In an essay in *Horsemen of the Apocalypse*, the 2000 essay collection, the designer Marc W. Miller described a common problem in 1970s war-gaming, the same era of American game design that relied heavily on depictions of World War II: "Players enjoyed the tactical level games and some developed a preference for playing the Germans. They transferred that enjoyment into other aspects of the German combatants and developed an affinity for the Nazi aspects of their chosen side. Without fully (or even) realizing the horrors that the Nazi mentality inflicted on humanity, they argued for the superiority of the Germans because of their weapons, or their organization, or their tactics, or their strategies. We called these people 'closet nazis.'" Though Miller claims that the development of fantasy role-playing "offered an alternative" for many of those closet Nazis, there are more of them than ever in American society, and they're starting to move out of the closet.

* * *

So is *Juden Raus* just a historical curio with little to say about how people are politically influenced, or does the very fact of the game's badness as a game make it *more* effective as propaganda? The "real" answer, as with most such arguments, is almost certainly a combination of both things, depending on the specific circumstances of play. As far as I can tell, nobody in my game group has become a closet Nazi. But *Juden Raus* is only the most highly concentrated game to invite players to become friendly with atrocity; if that game is boring with a background theme of deporting Jewish families, *Catan* is boring with a background theme of colonialism. While I would never choose to play *Juden Raus* the way we choose to play *Catan*, that's at least in part because *Juden Raus* isn't fun, and my lack of desire to play it is akin to my lack of desire to play *Candyland*. What if it *was* fun?

There isn't a necessary connection between the more visceral elements of playing a game and the parts that conspire to tell a story—they can work independently of each other, as when the game is fun but heavily abstracted (most Eurogames) or when the gameplay is sluggish but seeds an idea as being totally normal and deserving of repeated engagement (*Juden Raus*). But when the two strands are effectively woven together, games can become even more potent. That's because it's easier to be open to something when your guard is down; the Olympics, overwhelming public gatherings, and filmed hagiography speak to the way the Nazis understood this principle, though it was misapplied to *Juden Raus.*

Taken seriously in a burgeoning games market, this potential feels both intoxicating and slightly alarming. It's easy to imagine a modern board game that teaches children to seek out black and brown families before handing them over to border patrol. Many people in the world already live as if they were in such a game and take pride in their gruesome victories. This game would be treated by many people as an odd, slightly discomforting object, but it would be just the tip of a far more dangerous iceberg. America's closet Nazis are not hurting for games, but mass-producing ones that are as explicit as *Juden Raus*, and as comfortably stored in the home, has the feel of a shift in the boundaries around the player's life; this is the version of the world this person has chosen to live in, and, like proudly displaying a Confederate flag, casual play is a gesture indicating that it would be nearly impossible for us to occupy the same space.

Except, of course, we *are* living in the same world, a world that consists of and includes all of these systems operating at once, stacked on top of and next to and inside each other. *Juden Raus, Train,* even *Life* are all slices of the world. In each case, play models a small version of complicity, of the kinds of things we broadly acquiesce to every time we go out the front door. To play these games and think about them critically is to pull at the threads that weave together to create those systems and that create the wool that so often covers our eyes.

I didn't know any of this back in my college class. I couldn't have known what playing *Juden Raus* would actually be like—partly because the act of imagining *Juden Raus* is in many ways more titillating than actually playing it. But after learning about *Juden Raus*, my interest in investigating the potential unsung propagandistic influence of board games only grew when I learned about the propagandistic nature and bizarre intellectual history of one of America's foundational board games, one I'd actually played: *Monopoly*.

3

MONOPOLY **AND ITS CHILDREN**

If you ask someone who plays a lot of board games what they think of *Monopoly*, they will tell you that it is a bad game. They're right: It takes far too long to play, to the point where the board occasionally needs to be left out overnight. Players can be eliminated, which leaves them with nothing to do until the game ends besides needling the rest of the players and potentially trying to sneak their way back in. For a game intended to be played by children, the rules are rather complicated and vague, leading to many different sets of house play styles (for example, how your family treats Free Parking). And the end result is often entirely dependent on luck, based on who happens to land on the right spaces early in the game, enabling them to acquire a crucial monopoly. These are all true statements about *Monopoly*, but to harp on them in a conversation about the game is to miss the point—for anyone I've played *Monopoly* with in the past few years, the game's myriad flaws are features rather than bugs.

Each time I've played *Monopoly* in the past decade or so, it's been because one person really, really wanted to play—not one person specifically; people either have the *Monopoly* bug, or they don't, often depending on the way they related to the game as a child. (I don't, even though I played a decent amount of *Monopoly* as a kid, but I do enjoy playing because of how happy it makes people who do.) So few adults are willing to commit to a game of *Monopoly* that, on the rare occasions one actually happens, something about it feels special—especially for the person who made it happen. In my experience, this longtime staple of the family evening takes several hours to play (way too long to hold the interest of a child or even a patient adult), requires copious quantities of beer and substances, and is usually paired with a separate, casual activity—looking around a friend's new apartment, watching wrestling, gossiping about other people's relationships.

A seemingly endless session of *Monopoly* is, in many ways, the purest distillation of a board game's function as something to *do*, a way to structure your interactions with your family and friends. If you accept that the game is largely based on luck (or whoever cares the most about winning), and if players spend a lot of time between turns with nothing to do, then it's much easier to just hang out while playing without taking everything in the game so seriously. The variations of any given person's set of *Monopoly* rules—how people use Free Parking, whether a given family automatically auctions off property once someone lands on it, the allowance or prohibition of using out-of-game resources in trades—creates a myriad set of overlapping rituals, like the constellation of closely connected but distinct religious practices defining a sect.

Monopoly, at least in my experience, often has a special allure for people who are left out of its Wonder Bread framing of the world. *Monopoly* is an absurd form of capitalism in which everyone starts out with the same amount of money and, in theory, has the same chances of success in life. Putting this illusion into practice is an easy way to highlight what drives each person in a play session: the sitcom *Blackish* focused a 2018 episode entirely around a single game of *Monopoly*, which revealed the competitive stylings and personal hang-ups of the various characters involved in the game. It was a surprisingly effective, illuminating narrative device. And the otherwise clunky *Monopoly* is nothing if not surprisingly effective.

Hasbro, which has owned *Monopoly* since it acquired Parker Brothers in 1991, makes enormous sums of money by pumping out new versions with superficial themes every year: Alan Turing *Monopoly*, *Cars 2 Monopoly*, Horse Lovers' *Monopoly*. These are all the same game, of course, but there's a certain appeal to the thought of buying up properties that represent parts of your favorite TV show, your favorite band, a strong interest of yours, or another setting outside of the game's native Atlantic City. (If anyone is immune to the allure of Shrek *Monopoly*, I don't want to know about it.) Some other versions of *Monopoly* come with light rules changes: in 2018, Hasbro announced a "cheaters edition," which comes with cards encouraging players to do things like taking money from the bank or surreptitiously moving their competitors' pieces. Is it really cheating if the game encourages you to do it? Probably not—this is more of a "deceptive" edition of *Monopoly*. But hey, it's a market. And the "cheaters edition" of *Monopoly* comes closest to actually mirroring the original story of the game.

* * *

The earliest version of *Monopoly* was created by Elizabeth Magie, an educator and artist who invented what was then called *The Landlord's Game* and patented it in 1904 as a way of promoting the socialist single-tax doctrine of the economist Henry George. Though most of the original game's mechanics would be recognizable to contemporary *Monopoly* players, its ideological agenda is, more or less, directly opposed to what came later. One of *Monopoly*'s most salient features—that the game ends when one player has successfully become a monopolist by accumulating all of the wealth in the game—was introduced by Magie to show players who may not have been as lucky or aggressive during gameplay that such a ruthless capitalist system is fundamentally unjust. (*The Landlord's Game* originally had two sets of rules: the *Monopoly* version and one modeled after

George's ideas, in which the creation of wealth benefits everyone.)

After the initial release of *The Landlord's Game* in 1906, it became a popular folk game, frequently played on homemade boards with house rule tweaks by people all over the Eastern seaboard. Years later, a down-on-his-luck businessman named Charles Darrow discovered it when friends invited him to play in Atlantic City, where "the monopoly game" had taken off with the Quaker community. Darrow lifted his friend's board wholesale, including the misspelling of Atlantic City's Marven Gardens as "Marvin Gardens," took it to Parker Brothers, and, in 1935, successfully sold it as his own invention—completing *The Landlord's Game*'s transformation into the voracious, capitalistic staple of millions of American rec rooms. Many years later, the San Francisco State economics professor Ralph Anspach invented a game called *Anti-Monopoly*, which, in criticizing unthinking market economics, hewed far closer to the original intent of *The Landlord's Game*. When he was sued by Parker Brothers in 1974, Anspach engaged in a lengthy research process during which he unearthed Magie's role in creating *Monopoly*.

By this time, it was too late: *Monopoly*'s staggering popularity crowded out the board game market. The popularized version of *Monopoly* from the 1930s was far from the first game to include race elements or to use randomized dice rolls to move players around the board; *The Checkered Game of Life* did this, as did most other published board games at the time. It wasn't the first game to try to simulate markets; *Pit*, a popular card game first published in 1904, threw players into the commodity market and asked them to trade for wheat, rye, oats, corn, and so on, similarly rewarding players for being good at negotiating and playing at business. *Pit* was popular (it's been published many different times over the years), but it isn't, and never was, *Monopoly*. It might have helped that, unlike in *Pit*, *Monopoly* players begin with an equal amount of starting capital. Parker Brothers published *Monopoly* in 1935, in the midst of the Great Depression, when the appeal of acting out a rags-to-riches story in game form might have been obvious. The virtues rewarded by *Monopoly* in 1935 and the specific set of ideas embedded in the game from that time have remained part of global childhoods for decades.

When I learned about Magie's life and work, I briefly asked myself, What would the world's board game landscape look like if *Monopoly* had gone to press in its initial incarnation as *The Landlord's Game*? But that's a silly question; something as focused and anticapitalist as *The Landlord's Game* could never have achieved *Monopoly*'s level of ubiquity. Only a game endorsing rent-seeking, the practice of squeezing as much money as possible out of everyone who approaches *your* property, could be so effectively franchised. Instead, *The Landlord's Game* continues to operate as legend, a specter haunting the shelves at every game store. That might be part of why so many games try to pitch themselves as being the "real" version of *Monopoly*: most twentieth-century American message games—board games designed with the explicit purpose of teaching players about a specific social issue—are based on it.

* * *

Monopoly's secret history, researched and presented in Mary Pilon's 2015 book *The Monopolists*, is well-known in board game circles. But for the uninitiated, who may simply have grown up with copies of *Monopoly* at home, it comes as a revelation—the intellectual theft of *Monopoly*, the most popular board game in America, is foundational to the pastime, whether people know it or not. For the next several decades, designers looking to communicate something with their games relied on the iconic layout and gameplay of *Monopoly*, which created a shared reference point with players who might not have had the time or inclination to learn an entirely new rule set. Often, these designers felt emboldened in trying to get their message across after learning about the game's real history. It's a sort of localized creation myth, a hyperspecific board game Eden corrupted by a hungry, corporate serpent.

Take Bertell Ollman, a political science professor at New York University. Ollman was an unusual sight in the late 1970s—beyond his scruffy, sweatered appearance and generally bemused demeanor, he was an out and proud Marxist at the height of US Cold War paranoia. Though secure in his position at NYU (where he teaches to this day), Ollman was in the midst of facing real, professional consequences for his beliefs—he had briefly been named chair of the political science department at the University of Maryland, but his appointment was revoked under substantial political pressure from wealthy donors. In the midst of a years-long legal battle against the state of Maryland, Ollman cast around for another way of expressing his ideas. He eventually worked on another project that helped disseminate Marxism to the masses: *Class Struggle*, marketed as the world's first socialist board game.

Committed to being goofy and broad in his attempts to make his ideas palatable to the masses, Ollman went looking for a silly, low-key way to communicate the appeal of Marxism (sort of the obverse of the Nazis' obsession with spectacle). Eventually, he stumbled upon the concept of creating a board game. It would, of course, be reacting to *Monopoly*. As Ollman wrote in his memoir, *Class Struggle Is the Name of the Game: Confessions of a Marxist Businessman*, *Monopoly* was emblematic of the structure that made capitalism so odious. Even though it appears to give all comers an equal footing, "There is a real monopoly game going on, but you haven't been invited to play. More than likely, you could not afford the stakes." After months of looking for a socialist board game riffing on *Monopoly*, Ollman learned about the original history of *The Landlord's Game* from Anspach, and *Class Struggle* was born.

Spaces on the *Class Struggle* board are roughly divided between events that advantage the capitalists and ones that benefit the workers, as represented by the unscientific metric of assets and debits. Replacing the straightforward use of money as power in many games, assets and debits stand in for gains and losses in several different arenas of the struggle. The capitalists might get a leg up from more working-class people being placated by going to church (opium of the masses, etc.), while the workers gain assets from discovering common ground to build solidarity across race and gender divides. While the two major classes are the only ones that can technically win the class struggle—including a scenario in which the capitalists win by triggering nuclear war—the other players take on the role of invented minor classes, open to being swayed by either the workers or the capitalists.

Talking to me in his favorite diner near the NYU campus, Ollman freely admitted that his class division is a bit of a bastardization of Marx. But he set out to make a game that even a child could understand, and he succeeded admirably: the first full game of *Class Struggle* ever played included the ten-year-old daughter of two of Ollman's friends, playing as the workers against her father, who had been slotted into the role of the capitalists. At one point during the game, the girl loudly shouted at her father to protest his strike-breaking tactics. By the end of the game, she was demanding revolution instead of bedtime. Ollman admitted to me that this aspect of that first game was partially rigged; the girl's parents were fellow academics, and she was already steeped in the language of class struggle. Still, it presumably takes a lot for a board game to get a ten-year-old this excited about the prospect of seizing the means of production.

Ollman isn't a game designer by trade, and it shows—*Class Struggle* is occasionally boring, and some of the rules are so vague that they don't just require the players to agree on what they're doing in the style of *Train*; they make it almost impossible to play in the first place. When I played *Class Struggle*, huddled around a table in the back of a bookstore on another rainy day in February, the players spent just as much time debating the rules as my *Juden Raus* group did. This, even though *Class Struggle* was printed for mass audiences in the United States and across the globe in the 1970s, while *Juden Raus* had German rules from the 1930s and quite possibly never even got to the point where it was sold to the public. Unlike *Juden Raus*, it's hard to imagine *Class Struggle* remaining effective in a scenario in which the players' focus on the game has been dulled; the entire point of the game is to keep players enrapt within the circle, moving through and thinking about the different elements of its picture of class in the United States.

Thankfully, *Class Struggle* is very funny and enveloping as a narrative, which makes it easier to forgive some of the game's rough patches. One space that players might land on late in the game warns, "Government orders the destruction of all copies of dangerous game, *Class Struggle*. It may be too late however." One of the other players in my game remarked that Ollman must have had a high opinion of himself to write this. I have a hard time imagining him doing it with a straight face, though—beyond Ollman's sense of humor, the prospect of a board game single-handedly raising Americans' class consciousness to the point of revolution is a bit too ridiculous for even the most self-involved ideologues. Besides, the idea of using a board game to explore a real-life US class struggle is irresistible to a certain sort of person; lots of young leftists are aware of the game, even if they've never played it. *Class Struggle* might not be the most fun game to *play*, but it *is* very fun to talk about and to think about. That makes sense: Ollman might not be a great game designer, but he's a pro at getting media attention.

As articulated in Ollman's memoir, his experience with *Class Struggle* fits the beats of a familiar rise-and-fall narrative. There's the rush of having an exciting idea, the pitfalls of starting a new company, the heady days of potential business opportunities, followed by nagging problems with distribution and the finances of maintaining Class Struggle, Inc., breakdowns, and finally, the sale of the game to another company (the war-game maker Avalon Hill). And, of course, there's the press: Ollman went on *The Today Show* to talk about the game and, in the memoir, describes everything from radio interviews to live events where he played *Class Struggle* with skeptical capitalists. The *Class Struggle* story was so compelling, so recognizable, even to capitalists themselves, that Hollywood producers briefly considered making a cinematic adaptation. But *Class Struggle Is the Name of the Game* isn't just a standard set of tropes. It's also an effective meditation on the lengths Ollman needed to go to to get anyone to have conversations with him about class and to put himself in public places where people would take his ideas even somewhat seriously. The book opens with a quote from Plato that encapsulates the political power of games: "All legislators suppose that an alteration to children's games really is just a 'game.' . . . They don't appreciate that if children introduce novelties into their games, they'll inevitably turn out to be quite different people from the previous generation; being different, they'll demand a different kind of life, and that will then make them want new institutions and laws. . . . In fact, it's no exaggeration to say that this fellow [the game inventor] is the biggest menace that can ever afflict a state."

Class Struggle has lived on as a piece of apocrypha, a story passed around college dorm rooms and organizing meetings. After learning about the existence of the game during a post–*Juden Raus* research binge, I spent hours rummaging around online, trying to find a copy I could buy—or, at least, a set of photos that would make it possible for me to create my own version that I could then force my friends to play. (In an obvious and unfortunate irony, copies of *Class Struggle* online generally go for a few hundred dollars; Ollman is engaged in an ongoing project to digitize the components to make the game available for free.) Five years later, I found myself dreary-eyed in the back of a bookstore, playing an original copy of the game after kicking an old woman out of her seat. (We had the table reserved!) Sometimes, even in the socialist version of *Monopoly*, you have to be ruthless.

* * *

Monopoly's descendants have taken on a whole host of systems besides capitalism. Consider the 1970 game *Blacks & Whites*, a variation on *Monopoly* in which property is divided into an "integrated" zone, a "ghetto" zone, an "estate" zone, and a "suburban" zone. In this game, players choose whether to play as a white person or a black person, with corresponding changes to the rules—for example, black characters can't buy property in certain areas. As frustrating as it may seem to embody a black person in this game, there are some in-game "advantages": when a black character loses all of his money, he goes on "welfare" and gets to take $5,000 from each white player.

Blacks & Whites was a product of the magazine *Psychology Today*, which boasted a board game division throughout the early 1970s. The *Psychology Today* games, published by Dynamic Design Industries, were birthed by the University of California–Berkeley psychology professor Robert Sommer, who came up with the idea for a series of educational board games after observing his family engaging with more mainstream fare—in particular, *Monopoly*—in the 1950s. In an email to me, Sommer described the origin of *Blacks & Whites* as a reaction to "how unrealistic the board rules were, . . . everyone starting out with the same amount of money, being allowed to purchase property anywhere on the board (no restricted housing), etc."

Over the course of play-testing early versions of the game—originally an attempt at a more "realistic" version of *Monopoly*—it became clear to Sommer that black people, originally one of several minorities depicted in the game, were uniquely marginalized by rules surrounding housing and property, both incidentally in the game and in life. What had begun as a "realistic" attempt to depict US diversity in a *Monopoly*-style marketplace evolved into *Blacks & Whites*, a game that highlights how crucial (and frequently ignored) race is as a factor in who gets to buy and sell land. Sommer's notes from this time describe an extended play-test process of tweaking the rules surrounding race, trying to depict "how it is" by representing institutional racial bias in housing within the game. Under what conditions could people buy property, and how would they move through a system that was often openly hostile to the idea of their success? The play tests weren't always "accurate," which is to say that the process of creating a game to replicate the black experience had the unfortunate and entirely predictable side effect of replicating the biases of the white play testers and designers. In another unpublished note shared with me, Sommer describes the rules surrounding welfare as leading white players playing as black characters to give up on trying to accumulate property and wealth and turn welfare into "a way of life." (This "criticism" would eventually be made by an explicitly conservative and wildly racist 1980 game, which also loosely based itself on the layout of *Monopoly*: *Public Assistance: Why Bother Working for a Living?*)

Another *Psychology Today* game, 1971's *Woman & Man: The Classic Confrontation*, attempted to do for gender what *Blacks & Whites* did for race. The game's aesthetic, reminiscent of a series of exaggerated newspaper comic strips, features a woman "seductively" surrounded by panting men. In one space, a woman gets a five-point bonus for looking pretty; a man gets a ten-point bonus for working hard. (The game determines a winner by seeing who can get a promotion in the workplace first.) Women should take advantage of their natural assets, the game seems to suggest, here and in many of its chance cards—it's not like anything else is going to get these brutes to pay attention, either in the office or in the home. One of the ways female characters can gain a leg up on the male characters is by forcing them to engage in trivia about the history of women's movements: a sample question might ask which leader of a leftist organization said, "The only alliance I want with the National Organization of Women is in the bedroom." (It was Abbie Hoffman, in the late 1960s.)

The magazine's other projects from the early 1970s included *Who Can Beat Nixon?*, a game with a rather self-explanatory objective—to beat Nixon in a presidential election; *The Cities Game*, about navigating urban spaces via constant negotiation among the four player factions (business, government, slum dwellers, and agitators); and *Body Talk*, a game about developing the players' skills of nonverbal communication, all published in 1970. In 1971, Dynamic Design Industries published *Wine Cellar*, a game that claimed to solve the problem of not knowing the differences between different types of wine. (That these are all presented as equally important in the Dynamic Design catalogue says a lot about the priorities of "socially conscious" game designers at the time.)

How did people respond to these attempts at dice-based sociology? Writing for *Life* magazine in December 1970, Paul Trachtman identified what was, to him, the most important aspect of these games: they "give rich people a new insight into the problems of the poor." Was there a benefit to this kind of experience?

In each game Trachtman played, the players playing black characters won by "swapping property and sharing the bread," while all of the players playing white characters were only out for themselves. The only time the white characters were able to win? A game when, led by Trachtman, the white players decided to try playing with racism as their defining strategy, keeping "them" out of the neighborhood. The redlining worked: according to Trachtman, "It wasn't even a game." Eventually, Trachtman described himself as feeling "vicariously victimized by society" over the course of playing *Blacks & Whites*, to the point where his player group felt comfortable referring to each other with racial slurs "in good company."

* * *

While *Psychology Today* made games for adults, the primary market for board games at the time was, and is, children, who are much more susceptible to a designer's messaging—even if it's accidental. Just ask the inventors of *Mystery Date*, the 1965 game about trying to avoid dating a nerd ("dud") in favor of an attractive athlete, or *What Shall I Be?*, the 1966 game in which young girls determined their future career from options that included "charm school," "nursing school," and "ballet school." I played both of these games over the course of an afternoon, and, frankly, there are worse ways of learning about what kinds of role models mid-twentieth-century mass culture envisioned for young girls.

The premise of *Mystery Date* is simple: the player tries to collect matching cards that together make up the three parts of an outfit that one would wear on a date, whether that's the beach date, the skiing date, the formal-dance date, or the bowling date. Upon completing an outfit, the player can open a door at the center of the board, revealing a card; if she sees the boy dressed for the right date, they go out and she wins. If she sees one of the boys from the other dates, she has to spin the doorknob, randomizing the date card, and try again. If she gets the dud—a boy in shirtsleeves who my fellow players universally agreed was the most attractive by far, giving off a kind of *Rebel without a Cause* vibe—she has to give up some of her cards. Play continues in a sort of hazy monotone without much opportunity for any of the players to change the outcome, an accidentally appropriate way of modeling a courtship ritual in which a woman is supposed to be happy with whichever boy comes through the door as long as he's wearing the right clothes. *What Shall I Wear? A Fashion Game for Girls* is more of the same approach, though it gives players a few more possible dates and slightly more choice.

What Shall I Be? The Exciting Game of Career Girls asks players to move around the board collecting cards in order to successfully win the game by taking up one of the prescribed careers. The game gives girls the following options for the future: drama school, airline training school, ballet school, nursing school, charm school, and college. (The college girl is identified as smart by the globe she holds; her profession is "teacher.") To win, in these games, is to have the life prescribed for women at the time, complete with an attractive, successful husband who could make all of the decisions about how you spend your time. And, more specifically, the game asks you to aim for the life prescribed for upwardly mobile *white* women; in both games, there is only a single attempt at presenting a black woman, to say nothing of any other racial background.

The contrast between these games' attempts to ignore (or pay lip service) to race and *Blacks & Whites* says something about the limits of a laser-focused approach to identity-based games. For game designers at the time, it was exciting to isolate race *or* gender or any other aspect of a person's existence in order to make an abstracted idea of a person playable. But the decision to treat these aspects of a person's life as separate and capable of being understand on their own has its own implications for the way we think about them, even in the context of play. What would it look like to have games tracking race, gender, sexual identity, and other aspects of person's life rendered as systems, stacked on top of each other like an unstable *Jenga* tower? Do we even *want* to think of identity markers as being things that we play at? Marginalized people rarely, if ever, have the opportunity to put the box away and get up from the table.

* * *

The most distressing and grotesque of all *Monopoly*-inspired games is almost certainly *Public Assistance*. *Public Assistance* was created by Robert Johnson and Ronald Pramschufer, two libertarians from Annapolis who came up with the idea for their game while crabbing in June 1980. Together, they formed Hammerhead Enterprises, the company that eventually put out *Public Assistance* as well as *Capital Punishment*, a game in which players were asked to sneak "criminals" past liberals in order to get them into the electric chair.

Like most twentieth-century American political board games, *Public Assistance* riffed on the foundation established by *Monopoly*, with a splash of *Life*. In this case, players moved around the board, collecting cardboard cutouts representing illegitimate children, engaging in Saturday-night crime sprees (robbery, drug use, prostitution), and trying their hardest to avoid being caught in the Working Man's Rut, where they might be subjected to—god forbid—a union job.

Public Assistance aspires to be—and is!—simultaneously sexist, racist, anti-Semitic, and classist. Several cards suggest that welfare recipients can be enrolled in a "Judicare" program, which will set them up with pro bono help from an "ethnic" lawyer. Another card tells a player that his daughter has brought home an "ethnic" boyfriend and immediately forces said player to spend several hundred dollars in hospital bills after "the incident," to treat what are implied to be injuries from domestic violence.

The text in the game's rule book takes a similarly "light" touch with its subject matter, including sections describing a "welfare recipient" in Baltimore who reportedly had twenty-two "illegitimate children," "all by the age of 32!" By the end of the rule book, Johnson and Pramschufer suggest moving the game from one's living room into the real world: "Two players may decide to take this great game to the waiting room of their local welfare office and invite two real life able-bodied welfare recipients to join them in the game while they are waiting for their food stamps and welfare checks." By the end of 1980, Hammerhead had sold ten thousand copies of *Public Assistance*. Like Ollman before him, Johnson went on *The Today Show*.

Public Assistance attracted a sizable amount of public outcry, to the point where Patricia Harris, secretary of Health and Human Services under Jimmy Carter, gave a speech in which she criticized the game for being "callous, sexist, and racist" and engaging in a "vicious brand of stereotyping." As smart, witty libertarians, Johnson and Pramschufer used the ensuing press to respond with a line they continue to use in discussing *Public Assistance*, "We didn't invent this game, government liberals did. We just put it in a box." The pair themselves repeatedly admitted they knew nothing about the actual details of how public assistance worked. Instead, Johnson described the game in a 2009 blog post as being based on "street knowledge and common sense"—picked up, presumably, while crabbing.

Writing for the *Washington Post* in November 1980, Nicholas Lemann made an effort to fact-check the game's representation of welfare and found, unsurprisingly, that it had little basis in reality. Rather than the basic $500 a month that *Public Assistance* suggested would be given to an "able-bodied welfare recipient," Marylanders at the time would probably have received a fifth of that sum. Though the game tried to get players to think otherwise, most of the people on welfare programs in the United States were white, going on and off assistance as their life circumstances changed rather than remaining on a constant drip of assistance. "Life on welfare is not a lark," Lemann wrote, lightly scolding Johnson and Pramschufer for going too far in making their point. He went on to describe the game as "pleasantly racy." Lemann's most generous defense of *Public Assistance* was that it served as a sort of necessary outlet for "genuine feelings" of anger and frustration directed at the "perfect symbol" of welfare. In other words, *Public Assistance* was a game about "economic anxiety," the popular euphemism for lightly sublimated racism.

That same month, Stanley Brezenoff, administrator of the Human Resources Administration and Commissioner of Social Services of the City of New York, sent a letter to the CEOs of thirteen New York retailers, including FAO Schwartz and Macy's, expressing his disapproval of the game. "By perpetuating outdated myths," Brezenoff wrote, "I believe the 'Public

Assistance' game does a grave injustice to taxpayers and welfare clients alike; by its insensitivity and plain shoddiness, it is a discredit to those associated with its manufacture and marketing." The end of the letter read, "Your cooperation in keeping this game off the shelves of your stores would be a genuine public service." Naturally, Hammerhead sued.

The lawsuit named Brezenoff, as well as Mayor Ed Koch and the City of New York, for "alleged defamation, and interference with commercial relations and with free speech." The ensuing trial, which took place in 1982 at the federal district court for southern New York, was odd, to say the least. It included the testimony of a sketchily credentialed "investigative reporter" named Cathy Groudine, who claimed Brezenoff hid the existence of his letter to the CEOs from Hammerhead, simply because it was somewhat difficult for her to obtain a copy. (Brezenoff's office promptly provided one in response to a FOIA request.) The designers had publicly admitted that their goal was to "make people mad" to sell games.

Judge Milton Pollack decided in favor of Brezenoff (the suits against the mayor and City of New York had already been dismissed) on December 6, 1982, finding that the Hammerhead cofounders had opened themselves up to criticism by "injecting themselves into the welfare controversy for profit." Ironically, part of the reason Pollack ruled against Hammerhead was because the retailers that received the letter were not, in fact, threatened by its contents—many of the stores that received Brezenoff's letter ended up stocking the game in response to the publicity drummed up by the legal controversy. City administrators had no regulatory power capable of reining in these stores' exercise of free enterprise. At least at first, the people making decisions for these stores just didn't like the game.

Still, in a July 1981 interview with the magazine *Mother Jones* around the release of *Capital Punishment*, Johnson and Pramschufer complained about the nonexistent Brezenoff boycott. Among other things, they claimed that all of the stores that received the letter still stocked *Class Struggle*, a game they characterized as being about "overthrowing the government and not listening to your mother." Criticized for making a racist game about killing black people, Johnson told *Mother Jones*, "Black liberals just want to create racial issues so they can scare white people and stir up black people."

Is this really that big of a deal? After all, it was just a game: this is what Hammerhead executives claimed out of one side of their mouths when they repeated during the lawsuit that their game was a "spoof" and a "commercial satire," an idea that is hard to square with their simultaneous claims that *Public Assistance* was an effective and sharp form of political messaging—and that becomes even harder to believe after learning that Brezenoff first encountered the game at a cocktail party in Washington, DC, at the dawn of the Reagan era.

To engage with the history of *Public Assistance* is to see a forerunner of contemporary conservative media strategies—using a format commonly held to be frivolous as a way to shield against the implications of "serious" political speech, claiming the entire point of the project is to make a joke on the overly politically correct liberals, then becoming the aggrieved victims in an effort to drum up more attention in a largely sympathetic, blinkered press. Johnson and Pramschufer, now in their sixties, rereleased *Public Assistance* in 2011 with the new mascot "Obozo the Marxist Clown." (The pair continue to insist that they are not racists.) "We could have written a book to communicate our philosophy, but nobody reads anymore," Pramschufer said in that same 1981 *Mother Jones* interview. "So we put it in a box."

* * *

Class Struggle is, like *Public Assistance*, an idea packaged in a box, even if the idea is much more potent and thought through. Whereas *Public Assistance* uses the gleefully offensive images of cartoonish welfare recipients, the photo on the cover of the *Class Struggle* box shows a buff Karl Marx arm-wrestling with Nelson Rockefeller, in a giddily sloppy photo-editing job (Ollman stood in for Rockefeller for purposes of the photo shoot; Rockefeller's head is on his body). The comparatively low production value of these boxes is, ultimately, part of their charm.

The members of my *Class Struggle* group were acting out the class struggle, but the wooden stands and sketched-out art made it impossible to forget that we were, at best, doing just that: acting.

The tensest part of our *Class Struggle* game came, appropriately, toward the end. All of the minor classes, including myself, had joined in solidarity with the workers, and we were just waiting for an opportunity to activate the final revolution and win the game. My friend David, the actual owner of the copy of *Class Struggle*, playing as the capitalists, had amassed a much-larger collection of assets (the game's way of gauging each class's overall power), even though he was on a team by himself, competing against everyone else. At the last minute, David drew a card that allowed him to forcibly bring me over to his side, putting me in the uncomfortable position of having to collaborate with the capitalists when it mattered most and betray my partners. I was on the winning team with David, at the cost of being complicit with and implicated in the crimes of the capitalist overlords.

Board games can be, and often are, powerful. But the successes and (more often) failures of the many, many games taking up the challenge of *Monopoly* hint at the limits of what board games can and cannot do. When a didactic piece of art goes out of its way to *teach* someone something, it often can, at most, impart a certain piece of information: the system disadvantages black people looking to buy property; women have a harder time rising in the workplace. But the way people *respond* to that information is up to them, especially if the broader narrative of the game, and the exciting element of being embedded within a magic circle space, fails to sink in. On one hand, my *Class Struggle* experience made it possible to enjoy the victory of the capitalists. On the other hand, the victory was Pyrrhic.

In a 1993 piece published in the *New York Times* Style section, the writer Rick Marin attempted to give readers the lay of the land for the post–*Class Struggle* era of games. His piece included mention of a short-lived game called *Street Life: The Homeless Survival Game*, in which players engage in "Dumpster diving" and other similarly disreputable activities just to stay alive. John Ventimiglia, the game's inventor, reportedly came up with the concept while he was himself homeless, and he employed homeless people to make the first one thousand copies of the game. Marin also described games that struggled against the boundaries of the format altogether, like *The Transformation Game*, a game with no winner that provided a scaffold for players to work through a life issue in their own "personal game." Marin took these board games somewhat seriously but ultimately concluded, "Trend-pandering games are by nature ephemeral."

Marin's most powerful example was a game created in 1989, again based on *Monopoly* but with a much-smaller board, in which players had to roll and move to win auctions for luxury properties, ruthlessly fire their friends to knock them out of the running, and, if they were lucky, become the loneliest, wealthiest person at the top of a glitzy heap. Its name? *Trump: The Game.*

4

CAN FRIENDSHIP BE STRONGER THAN WAR GAMES?

A given person will associate many different words with the concept of board games—childish, emotionally warm, intense, complex—but one thing they almost always are is *competitive.* The entire point of *Monopoly* is to push everyone else out of the market and become the sole property owner in town. Chess, *Risk*, and every other war game in history exist to model a conflict, which any given player will either win or lose. *Catan*, which encourages negotiation and mutually beneficial moves, ultimately forces players to act decisively on their own to end the game. Even *Juden Raus* asks players to compete to be the *first* to complete their deportation of the city's Jewish population; the players may all have the same objective, but they're still trying to be the *best* at it. Why even play a game if not to prove you're better than the other players?

In this light, the rise of cooperative board games over the past fifteen years or so feels like a seismic shift in the medium, a sea change that might fundamentally alter the way people approach tabletop gaming. If your entire experience with board games comes from competitive games, it's hard to imagine what this might look like—the focus, objectives, and tension of most of your game sessions comes from everyone expending energy to *win* at the expense of everyone else. But cooperative games create a different kind of intensity: a shared frenzy in which the entire group assembled around the table works together to take down an enemy created by the game's rule set and achieve a shared objective.

Broadly speaking, cooperative games use cards, dice, or other rules to create an analog equivalent of a video game's artificial intelligence, an opponent that every person assembled around the table can work against in unison. For years, the closest things got to full cooperation in traditional board games were games in which a single player was pitted against everyone else in uneven teams. Take 1983's *Scotland Yard*, in which one player takes on the role of Mr. X, a fugitive from the titular law enforcement agency. Using a complicated series of bluffs, guesses, and hints, the rest of the players travel through London attempting to catch Mr. X; either Mr. X will win, or the rest of the players will. In some respects, this modeled the basic structure of role-playing games like *Dungeons & Dragons*, in which a party of player characters pursue their own aims while getting through the obstacles created by the Dungeon Master (DM).

All of the ogres, dragons, and evil wizards a party encounters are being created as collective opponents by the DM on an ongoing basis, windmills for the party to tilt at. And though that relationship can be adversarial, it's a cruel DM who goes out of their way to kill off player characters. An effective campaign relies on accomplishing the shared objective of world building, telling a thrilling story, and building tension, so that it's even more satisfying when the party finally achieves its aims. It's a group project, a sort of elaborate dance between the DM and the party in which the obstacles to the players' goals are difficult to surpass and the choices they have to make to pass them are even more difficult to make, but ultimately everyone—game master and players alike—is working toward the same thing.

In the early years of tabletop role-playing, not everyone could put together a full *D&D* campaign—or, at least, not everyone had a friend willing to put in the work needed to run a campaign. (From personal experience, I can attest that lots of people still don't.) So designers built solo dungeon adventures like 1979's *DeathMaze*, which eventually became cooperative, allowing several different adventurers to work through the same quest. In *DeathMaze*, players drew corridors and rooms from a random pool, placing them like dominoes to create a more or less unique dungeon during every trip. The rules take pains to tell the reader, "More than one player can win. *DeathMaze* is a cooperative, not competitive, game." Almost everything in *DeathMaze* is resolved through random chance, from combat to the special nature of potions (which can include alcohol) or spices (which can include cannabis). You're mostly just rolling dice. Using a computer, you could determine the outcome of a game of *DeathMaze* almost instantly, but the seeds of modern cooperative games are still visible—including the option to negotiate with the monsters you encounter rather than fighting them.

One of the earliest high-profile collaborative board games applied the basic principle of the genre—using mechanics and rules to stand in for a human antagonist—to a classic nonhuman enemy. The designer Reiner Knizia's 2000 *Lord of the Rings* game, which won a special Spiel des Jahres award the following year, puts the players in the position of hobbits seeking to destroy the One Ring; rather than having an additional person play as Sauron and the hordes of Mordor, the antagonists of J. R. R. Tolkien's trilogy, the game itself moves Sauron closer to the hobbits as they take turns, seeking to catch them before they end his rule over Middle Earth. An alternate version of this game in the vein of the one-against-many *Scotland Yard* would, of necessity, end with at least one loser, even if that loser was Sauron. In this new, cooperative version, either everyone wins or no one does.

Lord of the Rings was remarkable enough that Bruno Faidutti, the game designer behind "Post-Colonial *Catan*," called *Lord of the Rings* "the first collaborative game that really works." Graduate students at the Georgia Institute of Technology played it as part of a study of collaborative games and wrote up one especially interesting session. In this game, the person playing as the hobbit Pippin was carrying the Ring in the penultimate section of play, just before the party reached Mordor. Knowing that he was in a weaker position and liable to ruin things for the party, this player sacrificed himself to Sauron so that the player playing as Frodo, the triology's main protagonist, could take the Ring into Mordor unencumbered. The group won, and, as the writer put it, "every player rejoiced." The students concluded, "If such a moment of self-sacrifice is interesting as a story, it is even more engaging when you are the one to make the decision." Almost two decades after the game's release, more and more games have tried to create those kinds of moments, as cooperation has become one of the hotter trends in design. That's been especially true in the decade following the release of the most popular collaborative game ever: *Pandemic.*

* * *

In *Pandemic,* designed by Matt Leacock and originally published in 2008 by Z-Man Games, players become operatives for the Centers for Disease Control, tasked with combating the spread of four different diseases, represented by small plastic cubes that emit an erie glow if you place them in the right light. Here, the antagonist is the game's infection deck, which contains cards representing all of the cities that might suffer from *Pandemic*'s diseases. Normally, only a few cubes get placed each turn. But each time the players trigger what the game calls "epidemics"—mass spreads of the disease that increase the rate of infection and add new cities, stuffed to the gills with cubes—the discarded cards get shuffled and placed back on top of the deck, which means the same cities are infected over and over again. A good game of *Pandemic* is a miniature pressure cooker, creating an adrenaline-fueled race against time.

On any given turn, the players have a finite number of actions: they can move between cities, treat the disease by removing cubes, share information in the form of cards representing each of the game's cities, build research stations to allow for faster travel, and finally cure the diseases. (You need five cards of a given color to cure the disease, and cards can only be shared in the city they depict, meaning you need to do a lot of coordination to be in the right place at the right time if you want to win.) But the diseases move fast: each turn, the players have to flip over two or more of the game's infection cards, which add new cubes to the board. When more than three cubes are in a given city, there's an outbreak, which not only moves the players closer to losing the game (eight outbreaks and you're done) but also spills outward, placing more cubes in cities adjacent to the one suffering the outbreak. Get hit with bad luck on an infection deck pull and you'll spawn a chain reaction capable of ending the game in the blink of an eye.

A good game of *Pandemic* is like a frantic, multi-player game of *Tetris*. At any given moment, there are several crises threatening to take over the board: Beijing teetering on the edge of an outbreak, a low supply of yellow cubes, only a few cards left in the deck. There are three different ways to lose a game of *Pandemic* and only one way to win. In this intense environment, it's easy to miss things—a connection between two cities that will cause a chain reaction in case of an outbreak or the fact that getting to a research station in time to cure one of the diseases necessitates discarding one of the cards that made up part of the cure. If you're playing it right, the game slowly transforms into your own B-movie, with equally dramatic stakes. Imagine a scene in *Outbreak* or *Contagion* in which the government is forced to engage in desperate triage, allowing certain cities and people to fall victim to the outbreak in order to ultimately secure a cure and save humanity. From where I'm sitting, the strategizing that goes into an exciting game of *Pandemic* rivals that of any finely balanced Eurogame.

The full *Pandemic* experience can be intoxicating. In a really good session, everyone in the group stares at each other intently, unable to imagine anything else—or not caring to. (This is, in essence, what games theorists and developers are invoking with the term "magic circle.") Without having to devote most of your mental energy to scheming ways to defeat your fellow players, I've found, it's much easier to fully enter the mythical space of the magic circle. Except that you don't even need friends, really; it's possible to play *Pandemic* solo, since one dedicated player can float around the table taking moves for all of the different characters. But that very possibility—that the existence of a nonhuman opponent means you don't have to play with other humans—highlights a serious challenge for cooperative games.

* * *

The big problem with collaborative games tends to be what hobbyists call "quarterbacking," when one player who has played the game before, or at least is a more seasoned gamer, takes control of the session, dictating moves for everyone else in order to maximize the likelihood of winning. If you've ever worked on a group project or in an office where one person's personality and ideas took up all of the space in the room, you'll understand intuitively that quarterbacking can often make these games infuriating and deeply unfun. Sometimes the quarterback *does* know the best move, especially in cases in which they're the person who owns the game or has foisted it on their unsuspecting friends. But the fun part of a collaborative game is when the entire group figures out their strategy together and manages to experience a collective moment of breakthrough, with opportunities for everyone to contribute.

Quarterbacking chokes off the best elements of a collaborative game experience. But as a strategy, the rules of any given collaborative game frequently allow, and even encourage, quarterbacks: the enemies in a *Legend of Zelda* game are controlled by code that remains hidden by design, but the artificial intelligence in a board game has to be more or less transparent to the players in something like a deck of cards. The players, then, have to do the work in place of a video game's code. A sufficiently dedicated quarterback—say, a mathematically inclined, quantitative gamer—can come relatively close to "solving" a game like *Pandemic*, without having to worry about the other players' unpredictable strategies. In any given case, there's a *best* move, and the goal, in the mind of the quarterback, is to figure out what that is and impose it on the rest of the group. Preventing this is a problem for game designers trying to craft a better, more immersive play experience, as well as for the players. (If your game can be solved by one person, why even make a four-player game? Where's the fun in crafting an elaborate form of solitaire?) In the same way you want a competitive game to give everyone an equal chance to win, a collaborative game needs to give everyone a chance to *play*.

From this perspective, the existence of quarterbacking is also a strong argument against "winning" as the primary motive behind playing games, at least for anyone who's used to experiencing a quarterback. If the purpose of playing *Pandemic* was to win, wouldn't most groups strongly encourage quarterbacking or at least submit to the directives of the person who's most likely to lead the collective to victory? That way, at least, all players could say they won—*say* they won: it's unclear if someone in this situation truly wins the game on anything other than a technicality, the way a benched player might receive a championship ring that doesn't quite feel like it belongs to them. That quarterbacking situation isn't how any reasonable gameplay session actually shakes out. If one person tries to claim that degree of control, they're frequently subjected to a mutiny.

I've seen this up close and personal quite a few times . . . usually as the quarterback. Once I get into a game, I tend to become obsessive about it and *insist* that as many friends as possible at least *try* it, because they might like it. (After all, whom else would I play with?) *Pandemic* was a prime example: when I first got into it, some time in late 2015 or early 2016, I played hungrily with my friends who'd introduced me, until it was time to start indoctrinating other people. By then, my attempts to introduce friends to a new game had become well-honed routines. In these games, I would frequently use other people's turns to explain the rules—by taking their turn and giving off a triumphant, expectant, "here's how it's done" smirk.

Over time, it's gotten easier for me to leave winning moves on the table, only bringing them up to friends as teaching examples once the game has already ended. (Besides, I can usually play well enough to shore everything else up.) It's more important to me that a game go smoothly as a social experience than that my group wins, but it's still sometimes hard to resist the impulse to yell about how another player should obviously move to Cairo to exchange the city card and *definitely* shouldn't be building a research station in Khartoum.

Thankfully, as I've gotten more into cooperative games, I've found other options, including the *Pandemic* mobile app, which has transformed the game into a much more palatable solitaire experience. Playing *Pandemic* by myself without needing to set up the board or shuffle the deck feels like cheating in some sense, like you're not actually playing the game even though it shares the same set of rules. It's endlessly repetitive, since you can quickly quit if a game isn't going your way, and the rules remain quite pliable. It's a brute-force experience that's probably the closest I'll come to actually being able to "solve" *Pandemic*, largely by gaining a clearer sense of what the best move is in any given scenario. The biggest difference between the app and the analog game? Often, the best move is resetting and starting over. Playing on the app more closely resembles an experiment conducted with the rules of the game—with the opportunity to quit and try again using any of the *Pandemic* roles and several of the game's expansions, the app can act as a useful way to learn about the game. Hopefully, it will ultimately serve to make my actual games more fun.

* * *

The other reason quarterbacking is so frustrating is that it drains away some of the thrilling benefits of cooperative games, which frequently posit a model for how to achieve something like genuine solidarity. Competitive games often replicate zero-sum, or at least difficult-to-navigate, systems, areas of life where you're conditioned to take risks—real estate, financial markets, battlefields. Collaborative games can do the same thing, but in ways that suggest the possibility of shared struggle. What would it look like for all of us to operate in opposition to these frequently totalizing, oppressive systems—or at least for us to try to work through them in ways that help others, rather than hurting them?

One of my favorite collaborative games is 2015's *The Grizzled*, a game that asks players to enter the trenches of World War I as French soldiers. Throughout the game, the players go on missions, doing their best to make it through the trenches, but there's no killing and no combat. Instead, the players must endure the horrors of war. These are represented by several threats (missiles, bullets, gas), phobias, and traumas that stack on top of each other until the players can't take it anymore. The cards must be, more or less, evenly distributed—if one person takes on too much of the burden, everybody loses. In asking players to work together to make it through the slaughter, *The Grizzled* aims at fostering a much more intense sort of cooperation than even other collaborative games. The stakes may be high in *Lord of the Rings*, but here there's no magical Ring that promises to end the war in one fell swoop, only a vague promise of peace at the end of a dark tunnel. The game's tagline captures the appeal of cooperative games writ large: "Can friendship be stronger than war?"

The various potential traumas of *The Grizzled* are represented by a big stack of cards that the players need to run through in order survive. Over the course of a mission, the players allow these brutalities to fill up the play space, which doubles as the no-man's-land between the trenches. Each card brings the team ever closer to failure—players simply have to get the cards out on the table before the going gets too tough, with no recourse or ability to take the offensive. The tools to avoid destruction are few and far between, with options including making an inspirational speech (which protects everyone from one type of trauma for a single turn) or using a good-luck charm (mostly a one-time option, the type of random fluke that can allow a soldier to avoid death once but not twice). There's nothing the players can do to actually get rid of these traumas besides retreating when expedient to start a new mission. The team wins if they go through every card in the deck and make it out alive, revealing a peace card bearing the image of a dove that signals the end of the war. *The Grizzled* is more about endurance than it is about outright triumph; success requires the players to share the burden, taking on injuries and psychic scarring in equal measure: if just one player takes too many hits, everybody loses.

Playing *The Grizzled* is an immediate bonding experience, even when you play with strangers—as I did, the first time I played in a stranger's apartment while attending a board game meet-up for the Democratic Socialists of America. As a game about building solidarity, I thought the event would be a good opportunity to try out *The Grizzled*; though I haven't seen any of the people I played with since, it felt like I'd known them for weeks. Each session is about knowing when to retreat and when, though it seems impossible, to press on. (We lost that first game, partly because we didn't quite understand the rules and partly because *The Grizzled* is just a very hard game.) There's no way for the team to "win" any of the game's missions. Instead, you can only survive, strategically retreating in the hopes that the next mission might be the last.

Eventually, each player must withdraw from a given mission, activating what the game calls a support token. Each token is secretly directed at another player, whoever they think needs it most. When everyone has withdrawn, the mission ends, and players pass their support token to the intended recipient. If one player gets the majority of the tokens, they can remove a scar or recoup some scant resources.

If there's a tie for first—any tie at all—no one gets anything. Yet players are not allowed to communicate about what's in their hand or to whom they're giving their support tokens. Instead, everyone has to silently try to agree on who needs help.

Each game of *The Grizzled* is a dark, gripping session, nearly impossible to win. It's also, echoing and responding to Bruno Faidutti's criticism of *Catan* and most modern hobby games, the rare game that is effectively constructed around its theme: it would be impossible for a board game to truly capture the experience of being caught in the trenches, forced to hunker down with your buddies until the white flag finally flies, but *The Grizzled* makes a noble attempt. It's designed to create solidarity under pressure, to at least simulate the sensation of claustrophobia and an extended fight for survival.

In a sense, this is what all cooperative games try to engender in their players, but there's something special about the way *The Grizzled* succeeds at accomplishing it. Partly, this is because it's as close as a game can get to real life: *The Grizzled* names its characters after several people who fought in World War I with the French army; the designers are descended from some of those people. Tignous, one of the artists who worked on the game, was among those killed in the attack on the French magazine *Charlie Hebdo*.

The Grizzled is, I hope, just the beginning of what cooperative board games could look like as political art—the positive side of the power of games like *Juden Raus* and *Blacks & Whites*. Taken out of the realm of war, the tools of cooperative gaming can be applied to other problems that require negotiation, collaboration, and, above all, solidarity. Funded on Kickstarter in 2016, *Rise Up: The Game of People and Power* asks players to work together to build their movement while working against the nefarious, abstracted System in all its forms. The game gives players the opportunity to use the skeleton of the rules to model whatever movement they can think of, whether that's a fantasy scenario about dragons or the attempt to achieve climate or reproductive justice. Whereas boiling down structural racism or sexism is a recipe for grim, depressing games, doing the same thing to the dynamics of a popular movement gives young activists the opportunity to start to understand the benefits and pitfalls of different tactics, without having to live them first. It's early in the cooperative board games boom, but this might be one reason why they're so popular with younger gamers, who have begun to understand that the system that pits people against each other, and not your fellow players, is the true opponent.

* * *

As a game-design problem, quarterbacking—and all of the other questions about how to get players invested in a cooperative game without the promise of beating their friends—is representative of a central concern in gameplay: beginning to think about the rules of the game as a sort of leading guide, a group of genre conventions that can be subverted like the clichéd gunfight in a western or a last-minute rush to the airport at the end of a romantic comedy. For most of the spring and summer of 2018, my roommates and I were engrossed in *Sherlock Holmes: Consulting Detective*, an old cooperative game originally published in 1981. In *Consulting Detective*, players take on the role of members of the Baker Street Irregulars, the street urchins who serve as part of Sherlock Holmes's information network. The players are given the descriptions of the beginning of ten different mysteries, prompting them to begin engaging in their own detective work. The team chooses which leads to pursue by poring over the details of the case, cross-referencing the growing stash of information against the game's map of Victorian London and a version of the day's newspaper. Each new piece of the investigation will, ideally, produce a new piece of the crime, while other, smaller cases sprawl outward like subplots. But by the middle of our second case, we had spent almost an hour arguing about sword canes.

The three of us were holed up in our basement on a Sunday morning, surrounding the map of London on top of our coffee table, with a Lego figure representing our collective investigation moving from district to district. The collected editions of the *Times of London* had started to take over the majority of the floor, while I embedded myself into the couch, stuck my nose into my laptop, and wrote up our notes, lead by lead. We'd learned that the main witness to the crime had heard "the telltale sounds of swordplay" but that only one of the two rapiers on the victim's wall (because of course there were rapiers on the wall) had been deployed in the struggle. Although two blades clashed, the other was untouched. I immediately, giddily reached my conclusion: the witness had seen an elderly man walk into the victim's office. He was, undoubtedly, carrying a sword cane. "No way," my roommates replied. That would be insane, right?

Reader, it was a sword cane. The cases in *Sherlock Holmes: Consulting Detective* are enormously difficult and complicated, even for the smartest players and most attentive students of the detective genre— maybe especially for them. Following along with a mystery story is a fraught business for anyone trying to get the answer right, since the "right" answer largely depends on the whim of the author: two writers will rarely employ the same type of causality, the same understanding of what is important and what is an irrelevant detail. *Consulting Detective* works this way—in one case, we assumed that all of the evidence pointing at one character was, in fact, suggestive of a frame-up, since that's how this kind of story usually works. We were wrong. In another case, we strongly resisted the implication that hypnosis was involved in the commission of a crime—except that, of course, it was. The sword cane was, in short, representative of hours of conversations around the possible parameters for the solutions to any given case, a prime example of the problem surrounding reflexive engagement with the game's rules and the conditions of its creation, what is frequently called "metagaming."

Metagaming is, essentially, any discussion of the rules of the game that attempts to push against the walls created by the rules themselves: talking about talking about the game you're playing at that moment. Here's a simple example: collectible card games like *Magic: The Gathering* create thriving communities that move around changing play styles and around the freshest new cards. Sometimes, a particular type of deck or strategy may be in vogue, and knowing that, a smart player will build in elements to their deck that neutralize the popular strategies. On one level, it's just smart thinking. On another, it's thinking that occurs *outside* the rules of *Magic*. In some quarters, metagaming extends to using a player's knowledge of their competitors—personal habits, usual strategies, even long-term grudges. If a friend of yours tends to sucker everyone in your regular group by pretending to be weak, leading the rest of the players to gang up on them week after week, that's metagaming. If that same friend tries to change their tack in response, the metagame will simply go deeper.

In the case of *Consulting Detective*, the metagame is based on the tropes of the detective genre, rather than the simple artificial intelligence of *Pandemic*—but it's a difference in tone, rather than in the way you approach the metagame. Knowing the rules and how and why they exist is often more than enough to lead your party to victory. And if you follow the metagame far enough and for long enough, eventually it will turn any given game into a meaningless set of abstract shapes, like a word that's been repeated too many times until it loses all sense. Like words, the rules for a game are semiarbitrarily decided before we all agree to start using them in the same way. Negotiating specific rules at the margins like in *Train* is, in a sense, akin to the way words can have different meanings and uses in different contexts. ("In *this* house, we give people money when they land on Free Parking.") Getting around that sort of quarterbacking, whether it's based on someone's encyclopedic knowledge of Sir Arthur Conan Doyle or mastery of the *Pandemic* algorithm, is, essentially, a metagame problem—how do you stop one player's skill from overwhelming everyone else? There are a few different solutions.

* * *

Spirit Island, the anticolonialist game that both directly and indirectly critiques *Catan*, was published almost a decade after *Pandemic*. It solves the quarterbacking problem by making play insanely complicated. Each player's character—the spirit they are using to fight off the invaders—has its own highly specific set of strengths and weaknesses. Lightning's Swift Strike moves quickly, able to use all of its powers every other turn, while Vital Strength of the

Earth moves slowly, throwing up defensive barriers, and Ocean's Hungry Grasp operates by pushing and pulling the invaders into the otherwise unused sea spaces, drowning them in order to power its attacks. These endlessly multiplying specialized sets of rules make it hard to know how any two, three, or four spirits will interact in a given situation. Throw in the three or four *other* ways you can make the game harder, including different objectives or powers for the invaders, and, after a while, everything happening in a given game of *Spirit Island* can become downright dizzying.

This has the benefit of making it almost impossible for a player to tell the others what to do. Even if you're experienced, the best you can do is make gentle suggestions. Ultimately, the other players will have a better hold on their own spirits than you do, and taking control of a game forces the playing time up and up to the point where quarterbacking just becomes an impractical strategy. Like *Catan*, *Spirit Island* forces the players to invest so much mental energy in the game that it's hard to think about anything else: one session was staged as a break-in-case-of-emergency activity to distract one of my roommates from an unexpected and nasty breakup, combined with ample amounts of scotch, while two-player games clocked in at a breezy hour or so and felt as close to a before-bed ritual as we'd ever had in the apartment. Most of that mental energy is split between staring at the rules to figure out what *you* should do and working to effectively communicate the best way to stop the invaders, what *everyone* should do.

Other games succeed by taking the opposite tack and severely limiting the group's communication. *Hanabi* won the 2013 Spiel des Jahres, but it feels like a much-older game in the best possible way, like a lost folk game that's finally made its way back to the world. The odd conceit of *Hanabi* asks players to put together sets of fireworks represented by cards in several colors, numbered one through five. The players must play each of the cards out of their hands, playing each colored suit in numerical order, one to five, except that no one can see their own hand—all of your cards face outward, toward the other players. Hints, which allow players to tell someone else which of their cards are of a certain color or number, are a limited resource, and they don't necessarily help that much. (You might need to play a blue 2, but you have *three* blue cards in your hand. Which one is it?) The only way to get more hints is for players to discard cards, which, again, they have to do while flying blind. Even when you're totally in sync with the other players, there's a chance that, like in solitaire, the luck of the draw might damn you, or worse still, you might misinterpret the signals you're getting from the other players.

The Mind, published in 2018, boils this conceit down to its purest form: the players' objective is simply to place their hands of cards, printed with the numbers 1 through 100, in numerical order. That's it.

The twist here is that, while you can see your own hand, there's no communication allowed whatsoever. Instead, the players simply stare at each other in a form of purely psychological, barely perceptible suggestion involving direct eye contact and unavoidable hesitation about where and when to play your cards. You might have 27 in your hand, but what if the person across the hall from you has 26? There's no way to know. *The Mind* seems like it should be a silly and shallow, if fun, game. Instead, it was one of the most riveting things I'd played in months. Facilitating different ways of communicating, in addition to just different things to communicate *about*, is another possible benefit of cooperative board games.

* * *

Ironically, one of the best ways to get around the solvable quality of cooperative games is to reintroduce player opponents, which happens in semicooperative or "coopetition" games. Taking a different approach to the notion of coopetition than Eurogames, which require players to occasionally work together in order to emerge victorious, these games try to blur the boundaries between competition and playing well with others. Consider 2008's *Battlestar Galactica* board game, a widely beloved corporate tie-in game based on the television show that managed to take over my apartment for several months. In the *Battlestar* game, players are slotted into the roles of characters from the series: the gruff, reluctant military leader Admiral William Adama, President Laura Roslin, traitor-prophet Gaius Baltar, and so on. On each turn after the players act, the ship hits a crisis point, using a deck like the infection deck in *Pandemic*. These crises take many forms—a problem with the water supply, enemy Cylon ships attacking out of nowhere, terrorist threats—and the players have to secretly put in cards to pass the tests they pose. But there's a catch: some of the players are, or will be, hidden Cylons—in the parlance of the show, robots that assume human form, effectively infiltrating the fleet.

At the beginning of a game, each player may or may not be a human, depending on the loyalty card they have been dealt. But halfway through the *Galactica*'s journey (which is to say, halfway through the game), the rest of the loyalty cards get dealt out, and it becomes certain that one or more players are Cylons, even if they didn't know it at the outset. Players are put in an uncomfortable position: if they play well for most of the game, bringing the humans to a comfortable lead, they might eventually discover that they're a Cylon on the verge of losing.

Battlestar Galactica and other coopetition games like the popular *Betrayal at House on the Hill* play with the long-standing concept of hidden-role games. The best example of these games is probably *Werewolf*, a variant of the children's game Mafia. In this game, one or more players are given the role of the werewolf, hidden among the villagers. Each night, the werewolf kills and eats one of the villagers. The next day, the villagers deliberate on who they think is the werewolf, then vote to hang someone. If the victim is the werewolf, the villagers win; if not, the game continues. Various versions of *Werewolf* complicate the game, adding new roles and more complex ways of working together. (For example, the tanner, a villager who craves death, wins the game by tricking the other players into thinking that they are the werewolf.) Some players can win even if everyone else loses; sometimes a few can win under different conditions. In one popular hidden-role game, *Secret Hitler*, the liberals of Weimar-era Germany must form governments and root out the identity of Hitler and his fascist cronies.

With enough elbow grease and role-playing, even some competitive games can be turned into cooperative games. *Busted*, a 1970s game about selling marijuana, comes with the tag "crime does not pay." But *Busted* is, in fact, a game about making sure that crime *does* pay. Each player is an aspiring marijuana dealer, moving around the board, picking up a pound from the game's supplier, Mr. Big, and eventually trying to sell the product—to the other players—before retiring to the game's idyllic, pastel paradise: Marijuana Mountain. Meanwhile, the game's narc squad, composed of characters with names like Big Al, Big Boy Bob, and Muncie McKoy, tries to come after you. A group of fixers can give you special abilities—including offing the members of the narc squad, if you're willing to pay. In the game I played, on an otherwise bright, sunny day in April, we all did. Though we went into the game intent on taking each other down (and holding onto our money), eventually we'd murdered all of the members of the narc squad, and we were home free. Although *Busted* players can be eliminated, whether by being unable to pay Mr. Big or by getting arrested, it's also possible for everyone to win. All three of us successfully, blissfully retired to Marijuana Mountain.

By the end of the game, we'd created stories about our characters that were compelling enough to get us attached and invested in those characters, if only for an hour or two. We didn't want *anyone* to have to suffer at the hands of the cops, and our natural instinct was *not* to crush the other players, if we didn't have to—so we all shared in the loot and in the weed utopia we'd *earned* through repeated cop killings. It was truly a happy ending and a testament to how strong role-playing and narrative can be in even relatively simple games, as long as the game gives you some hooks to hang a story on. A game like *Pandemic* provides players with a puzzle, of course, and opportunities to engage in tactical thinking. But it also creates space *between* the rules, in which your pawns can represent whatever you want them to and the cities you're aiming to heal are constantly under attack. Within that space, the players work together not just to win the game (or to negotiate the rules) but to imaginatively determine what is happening.

Games aim to be *about* lots of different things, but our *Busted* experience—and the shared sense of ownership I've felt over most collaborative games I've played—indicates the way that games can also serve as malleable tools, capable of being twisted to be about whatever you want them to be about. Was my *Juden Raus* session about deporting Jewish families, attempting to engage with historical Nazi propaganda, or both? Probably both. The overlapping experiences of all of the players, and the intentions and actions of the designers, mesh together to form the story of any given game session. In collaborative games, those elements don't need to be exclusive: the designer gives the players the tools to tell their story, within the boundaries carefully established by the rules.

* * *

Why have collaborative games become so popular? I'm of many minds about the answer to this question, mostly because so many of the obvious answers feel, well, obvious. Board games are a market distinct from video games, for which there are far more options to let your competitive drive loose on your friends. Board games are associated with families and with togetherness, in a way that naturally lends itself to cooperation once that becomes a viable option. And a strain of American cultural criticism suggests that, at this particular moment, people have an ongoing hunger for *nice* things, for *The Great British*

Baking Show and videos of puppies and games that suggest that you might not have to fight anyone to get what you want. It'd be easy to dismiss this trend, but the underlying affect feels both telling and politically useful, especially in the way it manifests itself through games.

My instinct is, unsurprisingly, tied into what makes other ideologically motivated games compelling: board games are well suited to modeling and re-creating systems that define day-to-day life. Often, those systems pit people against each other in a frenzied, Hobbesian conflict; *Monopoly* may be a bit ridiculous, but on some level it is of course true that modern capitalism tends to enrich certain people (who are often already wealthy) at the expense of others. The wealth gap continues to widen, and billionaires' leverage over US politics has become increasingly visible, if not blatantly obvious. One of the largest and most daunting systems of all—the many scientific and ecological processes contributing to climate change—threatens the survival of humanity as a whole. Who has the people's interest at heart, really, if they are being fed into a system that can be easily replicated by a few dice?

The systems that prop up and maintain power tend to work by elevating some at the expense of others, assuming the winners will eagerly participate in the process of keeping everything running smoothly whether they're landlords who've more or less won a game of *Monopoly* or the executives milking profits from environmental disaster. But for more and more people, that is no longer the case. The revived, insurgent US Left suggests that working for the good of a collective might not be such a ridiculous idea anymore, whether that's in the form of surprise victories for socialist politicians, coalition-based action against the systems that inflict pain on others, or strikes that bring workers together into their own focused form of *Class Struggle*. Games often work best by offering players the opportunity to participate in creating a story. A story about people discovering the power of solidarity and coming together to topple cruel, callous systems of power feels far more appealing than the alternative.

But where do we go with the story, and how can it be applied to systems that *don't* just exist in static permutations? One of the more pernicious things about, say, modern capitalism is the way it easily assimilates any threat. (Cooperative board games are popular, which is to say they sell relatively well.) Another hot trend in game design right now takes this idea—that game designers offer players tools to tell a story within their created mechanics—and extends it to, if not its logical conclusion, then at least somewhere pretty close. These games are behemoths, inspiring a great deal of both awe and derision, and demand hours and weeks (if not months) of players' time. They manage to make even something as complicated as *Spirit Island* look like *Candyland*. They're enormous boxes-within-boxes, experiences that change the rules on players at a moment's notice, and they're some of the most exciting games being made right now, suggesting all manner of new possibilities for how board games can be organized across time and even across rule sets; and the best among them begin to point at ways that, through collective action and collaboration, we can beat the system: legacy games.

Note: Legacy games have plots and game mechanics that change as you play, which means that, unlike most board games, they can be spoiled for people who haven't played them yet. The next chapter contains some material that might be considered light spoilers for *Pandemic Legacy Seasons 1* and *2*, *Risk Legacy*, and *Seafall*.

5

LEGACY GAMES AND THE END
OF THE CAMPAIGN

"Well, at least we know not to take the placebos,"
someone said bitterly. It was cold comfort. Our
ragtag team had spent the month of July trying
to temporarily cure three of the deadly diseases
spreading across the *Pandemic* board. But the
fourth disease, untreatable at the moment, had
begun to transform its victims into lumbering,
zombie-like creatures. After searching through the
ruins of Istanbul, we'd encountered a virologist who
held the key to a cure. (She was the one who'd told
us that our government-provided antiviral drugs
were actually placebos.) We'd put up a good fight,
but by the end of the month, we'd lost. This was
my campaign's eighth game of *Pandemic Legacy*,
an expansive and ambitious upgrade of the original
Pandemic that consumed several weeks of my life
throughout the fall and winter of 2017, keeping me
in my living room for days at a time trying to figure
out the easiest way to cure the mutating diseases. It
remains the best, most thrilling experience I've had
playing a board game.

In *Pandemic Legacy*, designers Matt Leacock and Rob Daviau take the core idea of *Pandemic* and expand it to a grand scope, asking the players to struggle through a year of biological crisis for humanity. Each game represents a month of time, and no two months are the same—though the first game in January initially appears to be a typical game of *Pandemic*, midway through the game, the players discover that one of the diseases has mutated and can no longer be treated by normal means. It only gets worse from there. Each month builds on the foundation of the basic *Pandemic* game with new rules, new pieces, and new characters. Like in a well-constructed role-playing game, players are forced to reckon with the consequences of their past mistakes (an ill-timed outbreak in February can make it difficult to reach certain cities in July), to develop their characters (who gain relationships with other characters as the game progresses, including friendships, rivalries, and family connections), and to learn more about the world they inhabit (not everything is as it seems in the creation of the mutated disease). Unlike a role-playing game, however, there aren't really nonplayer characters—at least not ones you can interact with on a sustained basis—objectives are far less open-ended, and the mechanics are designed to overwhelm and facilitate play in equal measure.

The best thing about *Pandemic Legacy* is its near-seamless synthesis of narrative and mechanic—whereas the past hundred years of ideologically motivated games frequently put the rules at odds with the story, *Pandemic Legacy* blends them into a gripping experience (sort of like a version of *The Grizzled* that takes several weeks to finish and demands ongoing engagement from most of your friends). As you learn more information about the diseases and especially the mutated virus (named CoDA), the rules change, forcing your team to pursue different, smaller objectives in the course of winning or losing the campaign. For several months, you are given the option to accept help from the military, which makes dealing with CoDA much easier but comes with its own set of consequences. The group's access to funded events—special cards that provide assistance at pivotal moments—declines each time you win a game, because the government has decided you have the situation under control and can do without support. (Some of the game's models of real-life structures in public health are uncomfortably accurate.)

Most games are designed, intentionally or no, to reward repeat play as you master the rules. Endless head-butting with a rule system, like the hours I've sunk into the *Pandemic* app or my siblings' obsessive *Catan* games, allows the dedicated player to gain a competitive advantage over novices and clarifies the fault lines of the system the game is creating. *Pandemic Legacy*, however, keeps everyone on their toes—just as you think you've gotten a handle on where you should invest resources to effectively win the game, things will shift radically. As a cooperative game, it forces a team to work together in the face of the unknown. And it asks you to do things you're never supposed to do in a board game.

During *Pandemic Legacy*, players scratch off lottery-like cards to reveal new information and abilities, rip up other cards once they've finished serving their purpose, add permanent stickers to the board and rule book, and open up sealed boxes containing new pieces that have to be integrated into your setup for the rest of the campaign. It's a tactile pleasure that remains constantly new, located primarily in the taboo—you can't rip up a card in a board game, can you? This ephemerality, too, is part of the point: your group can only play through a copy of *Pandemic Legacy* once. If you lose, you lose.

I spent weeks thinking about my *Pandemic Legacy* campaign before buying the game and eventually hand-selected a team intended to maintain a constant roster of skilled players who were willing to hang out with me a bunch. That group splintered almost immediately after the first two games—eventually, my campaign encompassed friends, total strangers, and several games in which my roommate Jeff and I each controlled two characters, orchestrating cures, daring searches, and skin-of-our-teeth outbreak prevention several turns in advance. (If both players in a two-person cooperative game are quarterbacking, then no one is.) By the last few months of the campaign, a playlist full of Hans Zimmer and Cliff Martinez scores that I titled *"Pandemic* Boss Fight" hung over our apartment like an incredibly dramatic fog, darkening the space on top of our coffee table so that the board seemed to be the only thing in the room. The only thing we had left to do was mark out a section of the living room with masking tape and add a warning sign reading, "MAGIC CIRCLE HERE."

* * *

A campaign, or game that plays out over multiple sessions, is an old concept—war games frequently take several sessions, because players want to more accurately simulate an entire series of conflicts. (Role-playing gamers appropriated the word "campaign" for this purpose by taking it from war games, which in turn got it from military campaigns.) But legacy game campaigns have a more specific connotation. They're often built on the back of a previously existing game, taking a standardized, tight set of rules and drawing them out into something totally new. Each game in a legacy campaign has discrete rules, and you can win or lose that game, even if that's not the final result for your campaign.

The current, highly visible iteration of legacy games was spearheaded by Rob Daviau, a longtime designer at the game giant Hasbro. Finding ways to repackage the classics is a huge part of the work done at any giant board game company—it would be hard to sell hundreds of thousands of copies of *Monopoly* every year if there weren't new iterations to sell as novelty gifts. Sometimes, this need to produce gives designers the opportunity to tweak a solid foundation in exciting and new ways. (My favorite gaudy example of this is *Risk 2210 A.D.*, another game that Daviau worked on, in which players have the opportunity to strike their enemies from the moon or from underwater colonies, while navigating around a few areas of the world that have been rendered impassable by nuclear fallout.) Eventually, the need for in-house designers to experiment created the conditions that produced legacy games.

Daviau made a joke at work once: why do the characters of *Clue* keep getting invited back to the house every night? This is, in a sense, what you are doing each time you play another game of *Clue*. The joke paints a picture of a kind of Sartrean *No Exit*–style hell for Colonel Mustard, Professor Plum, and Miss Scarlet in which they are cursed to perennially attend this nightmarish, murderous party and never remember whodunnit. Though Daviau's initial pitch for a *Clue* variant that maintained a sense of history was ultimately rejected, he managed to get Hasbro's permission to design a new version of another old standby that changed the world map over time: 2011's *Risk Legacy*, which won several awards for innovation in game design and opened the industry up to *Pandemic Legacy*. (I haven't played *Risk Legacy* because I have self-respect and hate all variations on *Risk* without space warfare, but I'm sure it's fun if you like that sort of thing.)

The most infamous component of *Risk Legacy* is an envelope hidden underneath one of the parts of the box, labeled "do not open ever." The envelope contains one of a few different cards, randomized in any given box: some of the possibilities are bad for all players, some are bad only for the people present when the envelope is opened, and some are good for those people. There's no way to know which card is in a given box, meaning there's no way to game out whether you should open the envelope or be in the room when it happens. In a talk at the Game Designers Conference at 2017—the first year the conference hosted a Board Game Design Day—Daviau expressed surprise that most groups tend to assent to the effects of the card, even though they could just collectively decide to ignore it.

It's like a photo-negative version of the gaps in the rules that Brenda Romero explored in *Train*: even though everyone could theoretically simply agree not to accept the result of whatever's in the package, they tend to simply take it on as another part of the game, something they brought upon themselves by opening it. This appears to be an extension of the contract that is implicit in almost any tabletop game, enacted when the players sit down and agree to engage in play, and that is made explicit at the beginning of *Risk Legacy*. One of the first things the players do in any given campaign of *Risk Legacy* is sign the board under text that reads, "We, the undersigned, take full responsibility for the wars that are about to start, the decisions we will make, and the history we will write. Everything that is going to happen is going to happen because of us."

* * *

In interviews, Daviau frequently compares legacy games—or, at least, his legacy games—to seasons of television, with an ongoing story told in episodic bursts. This is an instructive comparison, especially from the person who created (and is attempting to popularize) the mechanic. Legacy games, like seasons of television, thrive on providing slight but significant variations on a central experience as a way of drawing out narrative tension. They court intense, long-term emotional engagement. And they thrive on twists—*Pandemic Legacy* is one of the only board games in existence that requires spoiler warnings.

Over the course of the years that Daviau worked on *Seafall*, the first legacy game that was not based on a previously existing product, the mechanic became one of the hotter things in game design: The popular Kickstarter game *Kingdom Death: Monster* asks players to establish an outpost in a blighted wasteland and survive, having children and fending off repeated attacks by terrifying creatures, over the course of twenty-five years, in an enormous box with exquisite (and expensive) miniatures. *Gloomhaven*, another Kickstarter game, sat atop the *BoardGameGeek* rankings for a while and creates a board-game-based dungeon-crawling experience.

Though not all of these label themselves as legacy games—as a marketing term, "legacy" most often refers to Daviau's games—they all share in the same basic mechanic.

In the run-up to *Seafall*'s release in late 2016, it got more press in nonhobby outlets than pretty much any new board game in recent memory: *Slate* called Daviau's work a "revolution" in tabletop games, while the *Guardian* described *Seafall* as "heralding a new era of board games." I can't blame those writers for being excited; *Seafall* purports to be epic in scope, leading players through years and years of exploration as their nations discover, colonize, and raid islands in the middle of a vast, unknown sea. It's an enormous box, featuring an astrolabe to keep track of time during a given session, several smaller boxes opened over the course of the campaign that contain new and exciting mechanics, and a choose-your-own-adventure-style logbook that adds a narrative component to each of the players' actions in the game—they might explore a tomb and risk the ire of a ghost, find a stash of ore or cloth, or upset the islands' natives and be forced to flee in the style of Jack Sparrow from *Pirates of the Caribbean.*

For weeks after *Seafall*'s release, I scoured sold-out board game stores for a copy until I finally stumbled on one in the hobby store near my parents' house during a trip to get new games to play with my sister. After getting a group together to agree to play, I was beyond psyched to crack open the *Seafall* box and do all of the tearing, stickering, and scribbling that I'd come to expect from legacy games. *Seafall* is expansive. It's also ridiculously, painfully boring. If *Pandemic Legacy* is *Breaking Bad*—a tight, thrilling series that tells a single story with a rotating cast of characters who benefit largely from audience projection—then *Seafall* is *Homeland*: an overly ambitious, plodding, ultimately failed experiment.

My *Seafall* campaign began in November 2016, a couple of months after the game's release. We went into our first session with bright eyes, gleefully tearing through the box to fully account for all of the envelopes, ships, coins, and decks that would inevitably come to provide scaffolding for an engaging, if long, play experience. It was not to be: our campaign ended in July 2018, after sixteen sessions that ranged from surprisingly pleasant to outright agonizing.

Unlike most other legacy games, *Seafall* doesn't have an endpoint determined by the number of games you have to play. Instead, a single objective—discover the island at the end of the world—triggers the endgame, and play simply continues until one or more players have the skills necessary to accomplish it. Though the game's rule book tells you that a group of players should expect to finish the campaign after twelve to fifteen games, the back page, designed to maintain records of each individual game, contains spaces for twenty, and as the campaign progresses, the elements that hook new players—the discovery of an unclaimed island, the acquisition of colonies, or a new addition to the game's trite mythology—come fewer and farther between.

Combining the open-ended nature of when things happen in *Seafall* with a few unclear pieces of text in the rules, and you have a recipe for disaster. (Online forums about *Seafall* are full of questions about some of these rules, which have the potential to totally derail a given campaign.) In our case, this led to a miasmic cluster of four or five games toward the end of the campaign in which nothing much really happened, like *World of Warcraft* players grinding their level by killing animals or *Pokémon* players slowly, painfully boosting their creatures' skills in anticipation of a final confrontation with the Elite Four. Some people find value in this kind of forced repetition, especially in a video game context, but it's a pretty demanding request to make of a group of five people who have to plan to be in the same place at the same time. By our tenth game (not including the prologue) in November 2017, we were at a point in the campaign where my very scientific estimation of pacing suggests we should have been by the sixth game.

In an interview with the video channel of the game store Team Covenant, Daviau describes his vision for *Seafall* as "Indiana Jones in the seventeenth century." "I want you to feel like Indiana Jones," he says, pushing for players to have the experience of "high adventure." "I want you to go out and feel the sea on your face." It's difficult to imagine an experience less conducive to feeling the figurative sea on your face than being clumped around a table, an hour and a half into a game of *Seafall* and only 40 percent finished, wandering around a Harlem living room and wondering whether there's a misprint in the rules that has ruined your entire campaign.

Still, the *Indiana Jones* comparison is apt—like *Indiana Jones*, *Seafall* uses its occasionally exciting mechanics and fights to paper over the repeated plunder of native lands. The captain's logbook that players use to track the narrative results of their actions invariably describes the "natives" as a singular group of people with little distinguishing personality. The closest the natives of any of the islands come to being characters in the game is when one of them shows up as a potential adviser to your province, someone you buy and keep stowed away in your vault. Even the most exciting legacy component of the game, in which players get to choose where islands go on the board by exploring the open ocean, communicates an unthinkingly colonialist perspective: the island couldn't possibly have been there until the (presumed) European rulers of the provinces actively worked to find it.

The obvious defense of this component of *Seafall* is that these are the tropes of the genre Daviau is riffing on, so of course he has to engage in them to some degree, to reproduce them to communicate the type of experience he wants you to have. None of the actual conquistadors or heroes of the age of exploration thought of the natives of the places they "discovered" as being real humans, so why would the characters in this game? Yet, somehow, all sorts of other genres have found ways of subverting or exploring the more callous parts of their DNA and of interrogating the pleasures they invite—*Spirit Island*, for example, demands some of the same moves as a *Catan*-style game, while still engaging in a critique of those narratives. *Seafall* takes place in an anachronistic setting full of mystical tombs, ghost pirates, and literal alchemy; it could probably afford to treat indigenous people as human beings.

A single piece of copy we encountered in our very last game attempts to reframe the players' actions; written from the natives' perspective, it suggests that all of the flat encounters from earlier in the campaign happened that way because the natives simply wanted to appease the colonial powers and move on. But this explanation comes too late and does too little to actually subvert the experience the players have been having. One moment of a game can be powerful, but it takes a lot more than a single paragraph, one that the players might not even encounter (the objective that triggers it is optional), to undo the cumulative effect of hours and hours.

That last game frustrated my *Seafall* group immensely, because it was *good*. Without spoiling too much of the story, all of us were given a shared objective with several different paths to completing it—rather than an ongoing slow war, that session became the most exciting type of race: against time and against the other players. During a debriefing conversation after the session ended, the members of my group agreed on a broad-strokes interpretation of what went wrong with *Seafall* and how it could be fixed: everything needed to be, if not more collaborative, then at least conducive to a different form of competition. Though we occasionally attacked other players to stop them from accomplishing an objective, *Seafall*'s mechanics incentivize players to specialize so that one person is good at exploring, another at raiding, a third at acquiring large quantities of gold. Eventually, only one person was positioned to achieve any given objective within the broader game on a reasonable time frame. Everyone wanted to open the cool new boxes more than they wanted to win. Racing to *explore* the world, and adding narrative consequences to some of the choices made earlier in the campaign, could have gone a long way toward making *Seafall* a powerful shared experience rather than something that left all of us, at best, conflicted.

Other elements of *Seafall* bolster the case for designing legacy games around collaboration, rather than competition. Whereas in a given game of *Pandemic Legacy* you can swap out players, even if they're still role-playing as different characters, the full group needs to be in place for every game of *Seafall*. (The rules lay out a system for playing when one person can't make a session, but that's no fun. It's not ideal to have someone sit out a *Pandemic Legacy* game, but at least in that scenario you're not messing with the competitive framework of the game; what you're really losing is just the opportunity to participate in the entirety of the campaign.) And though there were moments of genuine competition and attempts to raid or otherwise mess with the other players, we eventually fell into a common trap of legacy games: working to uncover everything and open all of the boxes, delving into all of the surprises the game had to offer rather than pursuing the ostensible goal of trying to win.

Daviau, for his part, views *Seafall* as a sort of rough draft of the kind of experience he wants people to have playing legacy games, a victim of problems with his publisher and the years-long play-testing process for a game of this size. Talking to me during a break from play tests for a new season of *Pandemic Legacy* and final preparations for the release of the legacy version of *Betrayal at House on the Hill*, he told me that he feels like the mixed reception to *Seafall* was partly because people expected something else from it and that many groups *did* pick up what he was putting down. (Based on the sheer number of message board posts about rule confusion, I'm not sure how much that's true; at the very least, this seems to suggest that the intended audience for *Seafall* was much smaller than the number of people who played it.) Regardless, he's interested in putting out a new version of the game once the rights revert to him, one in which he streamlines the campaign and focuses on the exploration component, in line with my group's experience. Daviau's attitude suggests that maybe we need to give the legacy game, or at least his attempts at designing them, a little more time: "I'm surprised by how many of the ideas I still like in it."

* * *

Are legacy games the future of board games, or even a format that will remain viable for more than a few years? Here the comparison to television—still a relatively young medium that has recently opened up to a flood of experimentation—is instructive, particularly as an example of a cultural form innovating and growing over time. Over time, television expanded from primarily episodic, single-serving storytelling into the multihour, heavily serialized shows that dominate cable networks and streaming services today. The pulp beginnings of the novel paved the way for self-reflexive, elaborate masterpieces. What would a canonical, classic board game look like in this vein? There are relative classics that newcomers to the hobby are encouraged to play; but most of them are about a decade old, and the pace at which games begin to seem irrelevant and outdated has only quickened. Legacy games captured my imagination in 2016; in 2019, when I write this, it already feels like I might be missing the boat by focusing on them.

As a storytelling format, even the few legacy games that have been released start to highlight the skeleton of the genre and what you can do with this type of game: each one I've played contains one effectively executed, cutting twist, often in service to the kind of story beat you might have found in *Train*—which is to say, in service of highlighting the way players throw themselves into a game and rule system without quite understanding what it is they're doing (a truth that is readily apparent in legacy games, in which huge parts of the game are literally kept in a sealed box while you work through the rest of it). Hours and hours of play can lead to lots of different, divergent stories being told within the framework of a single campaign, but they almost inevitably collapse down to a particular beat, designed to communicate a specific message, if they're designed to communicate anything at all. (In another Game Designers Conference talk, Daviau and Leacock compared plotting *Pandemic Legacy* to *Captain America: The Winter Soldier*, largely because they wanted to create the genre sense of a conspiracy thriller.)

It's no accident that installments of *Pandemic Legacy* are referred to as "seasons"; the designers want players to treat the game as, essentially, an extended television show that they get to participate in making. The first season of *Pandemic Legacy* does come the closest to realizing this vision, with its twists, its new challenges, and, best of all, its consequence engine. Decisions the players make in the early months of the year inevitably come back to haunt them, but this isn't a simple forced morality story about the bad choices you made. Instead, the game moves you from objective to objective in a way that ensures that, at some point in the year, your team will be woefully underprepared for a task, without feeling like that difficulty has been sprung on you arbitrarily.

But the story of *Pandemic Legacy* relies heavily on the players' familiarity with genre tropes. Leacock and Daviau note that the "plot" of the game is told in only twenty-three cards, arranged throughout the game's legacy deck. This is the simplest way to tell a story with a legacy mechanic, but it's not hard to imagine other ways that could happen. Experimentation and exploration in what you can do with a format comes over time and happens in a hundred different directions at once. In the talk at the Game Designers Conference 2017, Daviau traces the development of legacy games back to influences like *D&D*, early text adventures, and his experience working on an iteration of *Trivial Pursuit* focusing on the *Lord of the Rings* trilogy.

Throughout the talk, Daviau refers to "covenants" made between game designers and players, covenants that legacy games break—for example, that the designer is in control of materials and will not ask you to destroy any of them. Though I get an illicit thrill from ripping up cards and love tearing through a legacy game box, the response of many hobbyists has been irritation—irritation at having to ruin components, irritation at needing to learn new sets of rules each time you play, and, especially, irritation at the prospect of only being able to play the game "once." (As Daviau is fond of pointing out, you're *really* playing between twelve and fifteen times, which is more times than even intense hobbyists play many popular board games.) Though Daviau doesn't have firm ideas on what to do about these covenants beyond pointing out that they're enforced by the other players, whom he calls "unwitting co-designers," he is primarily interested in highlighting the ways in which he is trying to tweak them and wondering what it might look like to have them change and open up game design to more exciting, innovative rules and stories. One possible example might be the first sequel to a legacy game: *Pandemic Legacy Season Two*.

* * *

The second season of *Pandemic Legacy* is messier than the first. It takes place seventy years after the first installment, and, even if you won the first campaign, the world has not fared well. Floating havens distribute supplies to the remaining cities, supplies that are needed to fend off infection (now from one, single megaplague, the descendant of the first season's CoDA). As the staff of the havens, your team must add new cities to your supply grid, discover new areas of the world, and work to find a new potential cure, all while uncovering what, exactly, your leaders did during their exodus to the ominously named "Utopia." (It is a spoiler only in the broadest sense of

the word to note that Utopia is not exactly a benefi-
cent place.)

Season 2 essentially mirrors the mechanic of
base *Pandemic* by having players add cubes rather
than removing them, attempting to supply cities
so that they're ready to deal with infection when it
comes—again, through the use of the game's infection deck. Accordingly, as in *Seafall*, you're trying to
discover *more* of the board, rather than simply moving through the comparitively static story of the first
season; players use stickers to fill out a large space of
empty cardboard as the haven staff discovers more
outposts of survivors. And season 2 features some
legacy game side quests that make the final mission far easier, including additional characters with
new abilities you can uncover and use to inject fresh
blood into your campaign and, if you're my roommates and I, name after characters from *Frasier*.

Besides this inversion, the biggest change from the
first season is the addition of a lot more choice: in
any given month, the team can try to add cities to the
grid, open an entirely new section of the map, build
structures for strategic deployment later in the year,
or engage in searches, seeking information amid the
remnants of humanity. The game doesn't quite have
a handle on how to fully accommodate this full range
of choice, and so, like *Seafall*, the middle of *Pandemic Legacy Season Two* is a bit flabby. Still, there's
another reason *Pandemic Legacy Season Two* is fascinating: it's the game in which I've wondered the most

about the difference between my experience and that of other people who tried the same game.

Almost every conversation I've had about *Pandemic Legacy Season Two*, and every review I've ever read or watched online, has left me with a different impression. Some groups have complained that the campaign is far too hard, others that it's too easy. Some have praised the simplicity and ease of the central inversion of the original *Pandemic* mechanic; others have expressed concerns about the way it chokes off the game and starts things off in a very narrow, controlled spot. It's likely that these divergent reactions are a product of the choices you make about which areas of the world to explore first and where you direct your energy. It's the sort of game-design challenge that makes sense in, say, an open world video game, but that is here being incorporated into a static object—and while it's impressive, it's also pretty daunting to consider from the perspective of any given campaign.

Daviau's 2017 Game Designer's Conference talk tries to lay out a distinction between "repeatable" and "experiential" types of art, with books, movies, and TV on the "repeatable" side, plays on the "experiential" side, and board games somewhere in the middle. This is a useful guide for understanding what so many people find troubling about legacy games and why legacy games seem to threaten the idea of mastering a board over time. Critics of legacy games have a point about the difficulty of completely grasping the system, but they also misunderstand the nature of experiencing a game in time.

Even though board games like, say, Eurogames are theoretically endlessly repeatable, they still change *you* as you play them. You'll have a different experience of *Catan* every time, stepping back into the proverbial stream that is never the same twice, even if you're one of my siblings and you're playing against me for the hundredth time. Watching teen comedies is different for adolescents than it is as for adults, and there's no way to get around that.

* * *

Legacy games' biggest innovation is, simply, time. Turning the passage of time into a mechanic is what allows the designer to shift the rules constantly, to demand different activities of the players, and to tell different stories, all without breaking faith with what gamers expect and agree to going in. (For the most part—the game still has to be pleasurable to *play*, or at least it should be.) This change allows an almost entirely new dimension of gaming, or at least a significantly altered version of an old one. Legacy games haven't been around long enough to say definitively what their mechanics are best used for, but I have a proposal: providing an arena for players to continually negotiate and renegotiate the contract (or covenant) they enter into when they sit down to play a game. If static board games like *Blacks & Whites* and *Woman & Man* model slices of life, particular systems at a particular moment in time, legacy games give players the opportunity to engage with the ways those systems grow and change and respond to action.

What might it look like to turn *Monopoly* or its equivalent into a legacy game, where the winner of the first game has all of the money necessary to set up their children with a comfortable life and top-notch education in the next game? In such a campaign, temporalized so that each game features a new generation of characters, the well-off winners could buy whatever properties they wanted. (Maybe they would even start with hotels on all of their spaces.) The original losers would fall further and further behind, scrambling to be able to pay their inordinate rents accumulated just from landing on the spaces of players who got lucky a few weeks ago. They would go bankrupt faster and faster. By the fifth or sixth game, they might not even be able to move without losing all of their starting money. You might call this game *Capitalism*.

If that vision is too on the nose for you, I understand. But legacy game frameworks can easily be applied to other systems: the institutions of US government, Hollywood studios, publishing houses, sports teams, the police. Video games attempt versions of this kind of ongoing change with something like *Civilization*, in which a player controls their populace over the course of many, many years in-game, or even the franchise mode in a sports video game, in which the player can run through years' worth of seasons while still owning the same team. But putting everything in a box, as *Public Assistance* creator's Johnson and Pramschufer might put it, feels more potent, more open, in its ability to create encounters with these systems. Legacy games give the players, together, the opportunity to collectively negotiate whatever systems they depict in a face-to-face environment, where simply being present and agreeing to continue playing can constitute a strong statement, opening yourself up to the ongoing effects the game wants to have on you—and the ones you want to have on it. Which changes to the rules of the game reverberate most powerfully, and when?

This all puts the lie to one of the final themes of Daviau's talk: "consequence-free exploration." The *Indiana Jones*–style experience Daviau wants players to have in *Seafall* has a certain appeal, and there's something to be said for having a place to try out different ideas and genres. But in Daviau's insistence that players want to "try things that are conservative or radical," he accidentally invokes the inertia that defines games without strong, thought-out thematic grounding. When Bruno Faidutti criticized many board games for simply plundering historical archetypes for cool imagery and easy settings, he was making a critique of a certain conservatism inherent in those choices, the sort of conservatism that helps explain why *Monopoly* continues to be so popular decades after it was first published and long after it lost even the faintest resemblance to the way real estate works.

Board game designers have become wildly ambitious in the past few years, aiming at new and exciting formats for what board games can look like. It's not just collaborative games, Eurogames, or even legacy games: a Kickstarter in July 2018 successfully raised over $100,000 to support the *Edible Game Cookbook*, a cookbook that contains rules and directions for playing games that require cooking— whether that's digging a secret clue out of a cream puff or using your sense of taste to compete against your friends. With this rapid expansion of what board games can and cannot be, the onus is on both enthusiasts and designers to ensure we are seeing the kinds of games we want to play (or eat). It's not enough to simply rely on changes to rules and slight shifts in formatting to develop the medium; as games become a more popular form of expression— one that demands to be taken seriously—the culture around them must become more responsible.

There's nothing wrong with the idea that games give players an opportunity to try out different activities and modes of life; that's one of the best things about them. But when people are framing those options as either conservative or radical, as Daviau does, or when those options are mostly just conservative, as they are in reality, there's a problem: the conservative setting is, too often, the lazy one, the choice that doesn't do justice to the potential of game design as a way of thinking. Even when games *do* create scenarios like *Seafall*'s exploratory missions to "undiscovered" colonies, they still have the option to interrogate why, exactly, the player wants to try out just *this* mode of life—that structure of needling and questioning the player is already built into the genre, if only games were more willing to take advantage of it. To extend a game outward in time is to give players a myriad of perspectives for thinking about the changing systems and, ideally, to force them to think about what those changes mean in a way that, of necessity, expands the scope of what people can take away from a game. Legacy games asking the player to enter into an ongoing, negotiated agreement is, in theory, to create a space to learn. With enough elbow grease and imagination, it could be a way to allow players to try something truly radical.

6

GAME NIGHT

The recent explosion in the board game industry isn't just a function of *what* kinds of games people play—cooperative games, legacy games, games with explicit didactic motives—but also a function of *who* is playing. Hobby gaming is a hobby, in part, because it's something that's largely done with friends or other people who share your interest in the activity, in contrast to the family gaming that has dominated American living rooms for decades. While Euro-games are designed specifically with family play in mind, the simplicity and mind-numbing boredom of many American family games feels of a piece with the idealized flatness of the fantasy of American family life. Many families play *Catan* and other Euro-games now, of course, but that's often the result of one person in the family getting into more complex games and bringing them back to the household. Or, at least, that's what happened with me.

I played games with several different groups of friends over the course of working on this project: the group of Jewish people who agreed to join me for *Juden Raus*, women with an interest in how twentieth-century girls were taught to behave for

Mystery Date, my roommates for cooperative and legacy games, and a weekly group of more serious board gamers for almost everything else. But more than friends, my family—and, in particular, my siblings—presented a consistent, albeit occasionally forced, source of play. A huge part of the way I think about games has come from trying to port various games over from my friends to my family, whether that's in the context of an unpleasant, intense hospital visit or in an attempt to bond with my sister.

When my sister started high school, I made her watch *Freaks & Geeks*, the one-season NBC teen dramedy about navigating high school in Michigan in the 1980s, sort of my equivalent of giving an older-sibling lecture about what she could expect. One night that fall, we were talking on the phone, and she expressed an interest in the game that James Franco's character, Daniel Desario, plays at the end of the series: *Dungeons & Dragons*, which, like many gamers, he uses as a way to imagine another existence and another identity for himself—in this case, as the character Carlos the Dwarf. Since then, she's developed a healthy board game habit, as much as a teenager is capable of having in between homework, teaching freshmen how to write for the school newspaper, and being patient with me for a couple of years as I tried to learn how to watch *The Bachelor* and understand the complexities of reality TV.

My brother lived in Boston at the time, so my sister and I played two-player games when I was home.

Mostly, we played *Seven Wonders Duel*. *Seven Wonders Duel* is a sort of deck-building game based on *Seven Wonders*—a popular game in which players compete to build an ancient civilization while constructing powerful entities called Wonders. In *Duel*, players take turns selecting cards from a sort of pyramid structure (think solitaire), acquiring resources that can in turn be used to buy bigger buildings and, eventually, Wonders. The cards are randomly distributed in each of the three rounds, which serves to introduce a degree of chaos into the game: every session proceeds by its own initially established momentum, as players discover they've effectively set themselves up to build Wonders or buy specific cards—or left themselves in a tough spot, with few options for victory. During our very first game, I inadvertently collected six of the seven different symbols present on the game's science cards—which, as I learned while leafing through the rule book, is an independent victory condition. I had won, without having to finish the game or do any of the normal scoring or calculations for victory points.

Tensions ensued: my sister claimed that I had intentionally not told her about this rule in order to gain the advantage of surprise and win the game, and the subsequent argument has infected the tone of every game we've played since—not just of *Seven Wonders Duel* but of *Catan*, the *High School Musical* version of *Mystery Date*, and so on. I adamantly deny that I intentionally omitted the rule, but I'll admit that the moment was representative of some bigger problems in how to play new games, the competitive version of quarterbacking. Like many hardcore hobbyists, I enjoy using bizarre loopholes in the designers' rule system to carve a narrow path to victory, to try to figure out what the system is doing and how it can be exploited. But it takes different people different amounts of time to fully digest the rules of the game, to understand what it's asking you to do and adapt accordingly, and while my sister was (and continues to be) much smarter than I am in many ways, she was also fifteen the first time we played *Duel*.

The argument is far more important than whether or not I won the game. (Although, to be clear, I did.) The things I remember about our games aren't necessarily anything about the gameplay; they're the ways the games make the three of us approach our relationships and how we spend time together. Once, my brother and I were sitting at the kitchen table waiting to start when my sister walked into the kitchen carrying the *Catan* box, blasting the classic EDM track "Sandstorm" by Darude on her phone. Or there was the time that, after winning a game, she wrote "Sammy is the best at everything" on two sticky notes and put them on the doors to my brother's and my rooms, where they remain almost two years later. About six months after acquiring *Seven Wonders Duel*, I tried to open the packet of scorecards containing the history of our gameplay to read off the full record, prompting a series of groans from my sister. Why would you bring up the past, unless it was to indicate that she was winning?

A few months after my sister and I started playing *Seven Wonders Duel*, I wrote an article about board games to play if you were sick of *Catan*, roughly describing what could come next for people interested in delving deeper into the hobby—other ways of relating to games and situations in which certain games could be particularly engaging or useful. (For example, *Pandemic* was included as a cooperative game, an option for anyone sick of draining competition.) *Seven Wonders Duel* was included in this piece, labeled under the category "If you only have one friend." It's a two-player game, after all. When I posed the piece on my Facebook wall, my sister commented, "Just because you always lose in *Catan* doesn't mean everybody else has to stop playing." (She was right, although it would be nice to play another game every once in a while.) Later, she texted me a screenshot of the *Seven Wonders Duel* blurb with the caption, "Yes Eric, I am your only friend."

* * *

Many of the games that piqued my interest in the process of working on this book did so because they were novel. A board game about teens going on dates? Interesting. One about surviving the trenches in World War I? Fascinating! And one about the Holocaust? Still pretty compelling, if also a bit nauseating. Most of these games are, accordingly, good for one or two plays before their store of novelty has been exhausted and it doesn't feel rewarding to play anymore, before you have heard what the game is trying to tell you and can go on with your life. (This doesn't make them any less influential, necessarily; it all depends on when and where you're playing.) In these cases, the novelty and excitement largely comes from getting acquainted with the rule system, from coming to understand what the game expects from you and learning what it would mean to comply.

The sturdiest, most impressive games—*Catan*, *Hanabi*, *Pandemic*—are the ones that it's impossible *not* to play over and over, for which the game's expectations aren't quite so easy to pin down. To develop a long-term relationship with a board game is to tease out the intricacies of all the different ways it can nudge you and shape the way you approach a variety of situations and possible interactions with people. My siblings and I have played so many games of *Catan* that it feels like we've run into a wall again and again, albeit one that somehow manages to keep us coming back for more. This might seem to lessen the effect of other games, but, like all other cultural forms, the vast majority of games are chaff; you might watch a hack studio film once but retain certain choice images, in the way the experience of one single play of *Juden Raus* can stick with you long after you've put the board away. A game with a sense of longevity is, simply, the equivalent of a classic. *Catan* has long held that status in my family, in the same way a family might watch *The Princess Bride* every year or gather around the television to watch each new episode of *Game of Thrones.*

What would it look like for board games to receive similar attention to other cultural forms? All types of criticism are, in a sense, internal. Reviewing or writing about a piece of art necessitates engaging with the way it makes you feel and the experience you had with it, even if your argument is ultimately turned outward and employed to understand something broader about the world. Board games necessitate something even more revealing and more conscious of the ways in which the experience of gameplay is internal. I can review the rules and talk about the ways they appear balanced or compelling to *me*, but they won't actually *be* those things to me, or to others, if the people I'm playing with don't engage with them on good terms. In other words, for me to try to think about board games at length necessitates talking about my friends or, more specifically, to think about my family dynamic. I'm the oldest sibling, which puts me in a similar role to the quarterback in a collaborative game, the person whose learned knowledge and experience helps dictate how everyone else approaches complex problems. It means I'm the one who organizes many of my game sessions and the one who tries to steer them in specific directions—a tendency that helps explain what I'm getting out of games and why.

* * *

As we've seen, board games are much more internal than people think—the tapestry of experience that makes up one play session comes from all of the people playing, even if their impressions and feelings are totally at odds. But in a very real sense, games can use that inward focus to create an entire world, and, as we know, their influence can cut both ways. *Twilight Struggle*, one of the most popular hobby games of the past few decades, replicates the Cold War by structuring global politics as a series of contests in which the United States and USSR vie for influence in a zero-sum system. Besides reflecting the way real US historians and educators approach the Cold War (certainly, it's indicative of the way I was taught about the Cold War as a child), *Twilight Struggle* uses its streamlined system to flatten the consequences of revolution in Cuba, of conflict in the Middle East, of Soviet uprisings, using all of those components to get the player to think about every aspect of world politics solely based on the way it influences a great power, externalized and represented by the player as more of a corporation than a thriving nation. The people at the margins are left in the box.

It's easy to imagine becoming intoxicated by the appeal of this kind of game—the designers of *Twilight Struggle* work as lobbyists and essentially translate their biases and political framework into a game system that has gone on to influence thousands of people. The 2010 game *Labyrinth* takes a similar approach to ongoing global conflict by depicting the endless War on Terror, asking players to take on similarly abstracted roles as either the United States or Islamic jihadists (a very different type of *Class Struggle*). But it's also possible to consider these distilled systems as teaching tools that highlight the very *limitations* of their approaches. If US diplomats and strategists essentially approached real-world international relations as a game of *Twilight Struggle*, what would it look like to live in a world where we all tried to play a different game?

I wouldn't know, because my family refuses to play anything except *Catan*. Sure, we've tried things on occasion, but none of them have stuck. We went through exactly one session of *Pandemic* once, then stopped—if there was no way for any of us to win, why would we even play? Other games like *Bohnanza*, *Forbidden Island*, and even *Scrabble* simply don't create the dynamic the three of us are looking for when we sit down at a table to play. (The closest we've come is *Monopoly Deal*, a quick-paced card game that allows us to try to crush each other while on the road and in even less time.) When I looked through the *Seven Wonders Duel* results packet, the sheer number of times my sister and I had played started to make the game feel like a private language, one that we were playing for reasons unknown to anyone else. Games can pull us in different directions, but they inevitably come up against the tendencies of the players.

In the beginning of Ollman's *Class Struggle* memoir, he tries to describe the process of falling into the world of board games. While he did discover a lengthy history of "message" games and ways that games can be used to influence people, he also learned that the reason games can be so potent is precisely because of the qualities that are hardest to control, whether as a designer or a player. Board games, he says, are an entirely magical, new place: "a fairy land where fun is king and everybody his subject."

Gameography

Design credits are frequently left out of the box or rule packets for older board games, while the publication history for games that began as traditional folk games is often murky, and some games can go through many different publishers over the course of a number of years. Citation for games cited or played prioritizes the initial publisher of a game and is the best available information, often collected with the help of the online board game resource *Board Game Geek*.

Anti-Monopoly	Created by Ralph Anspach. Ages 8+. Anti-Monopoly Inc., 1973.
Axis & Allies	Created by Larry Harris Jr. Ages 12+ Nova Game Designs, 1981.
Azul	Created by Michael Kiesling. Ages 8+. Next Move Games, 2017.
Bananagrams	Created by Rena Nathanson and Abe Nathanson. Bananagrams Inc., 2006.
Battleship	Traditional pen-and-paper game. Milton Bradley, 1967.
Battlestar Galactica: The Board Game	Created by Corey Konieczka. Ages 10+. Fantasy Flight Games, 2008.

Betrayal at House on the Hill	Created by Rob Daviau, Bruce Glassco, Bill McQuillan, Mike Selinker, and Teeuwynn Woodruff. Ages 10+. Avalon Hill, 2004.
Betrayal Legacy	Created by Rob Daviau, Noah Cohen, J. R. Honeycutt, Ryan Miller, Brian Neff, and Andrew Veen. Ages 12+. Avalon Hill, 2018.
Blacks & Whites	Created by Robert Sommer and Judy Tart. Dynamic Designs, 1970.
Body Talk	Created by Layne A. Longfellow, Terry Van Orshoven, Anthony Rose, and Martin Thommes. Ages 16+. Dynamic Designs, 1970.
Bohnanza	Created by Uwe Rosenberg. Ages 13+ Amigo Spiele, 1997.
Busted: Crime Does Not Pay	Created by Richard Matto. Busted LLC, 1976.
Candyland	Created by Eleanor Abbott. Ages 3+. Hasbro, 1949.
Capital Punishment	Created by Robert Johnson and Ronald Pramschufer. Hammerhead Enterprises, 1981.
Catan	Created by Klaus Teuber. Ages 10+. Mayfair Games, 1995.
The Checkered Game of Life	Created by Milton Bradley. Milton Bradley, 1860.
Chutes & Ladders	Traditional folk game.
Class Struggle	Created by Bertell Ollman. Ages 12+. Class Struggle Inc., 1978.

Clue	Created by Anthony Pratt. Ages 8+. Waddingtons, 1949.
Collateral Damage	Created by Matthew Duhan. Gozer Games LLC, 2007.
Consentacle	Created by Naomi Clark. Ages 18+. Self-published, 2014.
DeathMaze	Created by Greg Costikyan. Ages 10+. Encore, 1979.
Fang Den Hut	Created by C. A. N. Neves. Ages 6+. Verlag Volk und Bild, 1927.
Flamme Rouge	Created by Asger Harding Granerud. Ages 8+. Stronghold Games, 2016.
Forbidden Island	Created by Matt Leacock. Ages 10+. Gamewright, 2010.
The Funny Game of Hit or Miss	McLoughlin Bros., ca. 1900.
Game of Mail, Express, or Accommodation	McLoughlin Bros., 1895.
Game of the North Pole	McLoughlin Bros., 1897.
Ghost Pirates	Created by Tim Rodriguez. Ages 13+. Brooklyn Indie Games, 2012.
Gloomhaven	Created by Isaac Childres. Ages 12+. Cephalofair Games, 2017.
The Grizzled	Created by Fabien Riffaud and Juan Rodriguez. Ages 14+. Sweet Games, 2015.
Hanabi	Created by Antoine Bauza. Ages 8+. Asmodee, 2010.

Harassment: You Be the Judge	Created by Larry Balsamo, and Sandra Bergeson. Ages 10+. TDC Games, 1992.
The International Mail: An Instructive Game	J. W. Spears and Sons, ca. 1910.
Istanbul	Created by Rüdiger Dorn. Ages 10+. Pegasus Spiele, 2014.
Juden Raus	Unknown.
Karmaka	Created by Eddy Boxerman and Dave Burke. Ages 13+. Hemisphere Games, 2016.
Kingdom Death: Monster	Created by Adam Poots. Ages 17+. Kingdom Death, 2015.
King of Tokyo	Created by Richard Garfield. Ages 8+. IELLO, 2011.
Labyrinth	Created by Volko Ruhnke. Ages 12+. GMT Games, 2010.
The Landlord's Game	Created by Elizabeth Magie. Ages 10+. Self-published, 1904.
Life	Created by Reuben Klamer and Bill Markham. Ages 8+. Milton Bradley, 1960.
Lord of the Rings	Created by Reiner Knizia. Ages 12+. Kosmos, 2000.
Magic: The Gathering	Created by Richard Garfield. Ages 13+. Wizards of the Coast, 1993.
Magical Athlete	Created by Takashi Ishida. Ages 9+. Z-Man Games, 2002.

The Mind	Created by Wolfgang Warsch. Ages 8+. Nürnberger-Spielkarten-Verlag, 2018.
Monopoly	Created by Charles Darrow. Ages 8+. Parker Brothers, 1933.
Monopoly Deal	Created by Katharine Chapman. Ages 8+. Parker Brothers, 2008.
Mr. T: The Game	Ages 6+. Milton Bradley, 1983.
Munchkin	Created by Steve Jackson. Ages 10+. Steve Jackson Games, 2001.
Mystery Date	Created by Marvin Glass. Ages 7+. Milton Bradley, 1965.
The New World	Created by Brenda Romero. 2008.
Operation	Created by Marvin Glass and John Spinello. Ages 6+. Milton Bradley, 1965.
Pandemic	Created by Matt Leacock. Ages 8+. Z-Man Games, 2008.
Pandemic Legacy: Season 1	Created by Rob Daviau and Matt Leacock. Ages 13+. Z-Man Games, 2015.
Pandemic Legacy Season 2	Created Rob Daviau and Matt Leacock. Ages 14+. Z-Man Games, 2017.
Patchwork	Created by Uwe Rosenberg. Ages 8+. Mayfair Games, 2014.
Pit	Created by Edgar Cayce. Ages 7+. Parker Brothers, 1903.
Public Assistance	Created by Robert Johnson and Ronald Pramschufer. Ages 18+. Hammerhead Enterprises, 1980.

Queendomino	Created by Bruno Cathala. Ages 8+. Blackrock Games, 2017.
Rise Up: The Game of People and Power	Created by Brian Van Slyke. Ages 10+. Toolbox for Education and Social Action, 2017.
Risk	Created by Albert Lamorisse and Michael I. Levin. Ages 10+. Parker Brothers, 1959.
Risk Legacy	Created by Rob Daviau and Chris Dupuis. Ages 13+. Hasbro, 2011.
Risk 2210 A.D.	Created by Rob Daviau and Craig Van Ness. Ages 10+. Avalon Hill, 2001.
Road to the White House	Created by Jim Musser. Ages 12+. Mayfair Games, 1992.
Scotland Yard	Created by Manfred Burggraf, Dorothy Garrels, Wolf Hoermann, Fritz Ifland, Werner Scheerer, and Werner Schlegel. Ages 10+. Ravensburger, 1983.
Scrabble	Created by Alfred Mosher Butts. Ages 10+. Selchow and Righter, 1948.
Seafall	Created by Rob Daviau. Ages 14+. Plaid Hat Games, 2016.
Secret Hitler	Created by Mike Boxleiter, Tommy Maranges, and Max Temkin. Ages 13+. Goat Wolf & Cabbage, 2016.
Seven Wonders	Created by Antoine Bauza. Ages 10+. Repos Production, 2010.
Seven Wonders Duel	Created by Antoine Bauza and Bruno Cathala. Ages 10+. Repos Production, 2015.

Sherlock Holmes: Consulting Detective	Created by Raymond Edwards, Suzanne Goldberg, and Gary Grady. Ages 10+. Sleuth Publications, 1981.
Smash Up	Created by Paul Peterson. Ages 12+. Alderac Entertainment Group, 2012.
Spirit Island	Created by R. Eric Reuss. Ages 13+. Greater Than Games, 2017.
Splendor	Created by Marc André. Ages 10+. Space Cowboys, 2014.
Stratego	Created by Jacques Johan Mogendorff. Ages 8+. Carlit, 1946.
Street Life: The Homeless Survival Game	Created by John Ventimiglia. Ages 12+. Anyone Can Par Inc., 1992.
Terraforming Mars	Created by Jacob Fryxelius. Ages 12+. FryxGames, 2016.
T.I.M.E. Stories	Created by Peggy Chassenet and Manuel Rozoy. Ages 12+. Space Cowboys, 2015.
Train	Created by Brenda Romero. 2009.
Trivial Pursuit: Lord of the Rings Trilogy Edition	DVD. Hasbro, 2004.
Trump: The Game	Created by Jeffrey Breslow, Howard J. Morrison, and Rouben Terzian. Ages 12+. Milton Bradley, 1989.
Twilight Struggle	Created by Ananda Gupta and Jason Matthews. Ages 13+. GMT Games, 2005.

Werewolf	Created by Dimitry Davidoff and Andrew Plotkin. Ages 8+. 1986.
What Shall I Wear?	Ages 7+. Selchow and Righter, 1969.
Who Can Beat Nixon?	Ages 7+. Dynamic Designs, 1970.
Wine Cellar	Dynamic Designs, 1971.
Woman & Man: The Classic Confrontation	Dynamic Designs, 1971.

About the Author

Eric Thurm is a writer whose work has appeared in, among other publications, *Esquire*, *Wired*, *Real Life*, and the *New York Times*.

Printed in the United States
By Bookmasters